Voice's Daughter of a Heart Yet to Be Born

VOICE'S DAUGHTER OF A HEART YET TO BE BORN

ANNE WALDMAN

Coffee House Press
Minneapolis
2016

Coffee House Press books are available to the trade through our primary distributor, Consortium Book Sales & Distribution, cbsd.com or (800) 283-3572. For personal orders, catalogs, or other information, write to info@coffeehousepress.org.

Coffee House Press is a nonprofit literary publishing house. Support from private foundations, corporate giving programs, government programs, and generous individuals helps make the publication of our books possible. We gratefully acknowledge their support in detail in the back of this book.

LIBRARY OF CONGRESS CATALOGING-IN-PUBLICATION DATA

Names: Waldman, Anne, 1945– author.
Title: Voice's daughter of a heart yet to be born / Anne Waldman.
Description: Minneapolis : Coffee House Press, 2016.
Identifiers: LCCN 2015043097 | ISBN 9781566894388 (paperback)
Subjects: | BISAC: POETRY / American / General. | POETRY / Ancient, Classical
   & Medieval.
Classification: LCC PS3573.A4215 A6 2016 | DDC 811/.54—dc23
LC record available at http://lccn.loc.gov/2015043097

Acknowledgments

A section of this book, "Offworld," was previously published in *Conjunctions* and has been recorded by Fast Speaking Music. "Citadels Thel Leaves Ringing" appeared in the *Denver Quarterly,* a segment from "Endtime" was included on the Poem-a-Day website from the Academy of American Poets, and "Dear Locator" has been published in the *Brooklyn Rail.*

The images on the cover and throughout the book are of a sculpture entitled *Girl* by Kiki Smith, 2014. Reproduced courtesy of the artist and Pace Gallery.

The painting depicted in "Threads" is *Thel leaning over the 'Matron Clay' and the worm* by William Blake, © The Trustees of the British Museum. Reproduced with permission.

Self-portaits by the author.

Thanks to Gillian McCain, Mei-mei Berssenbrugge, Kiki Smith, Sarah Riggs, Alystyre Julian, Pat Steir, Claudia Rankine, and the Guggenheim Memorial Foundation. And to Ed Bowes and Reed Bye. Special thanks to my editor, Erika Stevens.

Gratitude to Will Alexander for his evocative phrase "Urn Singer."

PRINTED IN THE UNITED STATES OF AMERICA

23 22 21 20 19 18 17 16   1 2 3 4 5 6 7 8

—for Althea Schelling
a very present daughter

A voice comes to one in the dark. Imagine.

—Samuel Beckett

Dost thou O little Cloud? I fear that I am not like thee;
For I walk through the vales of Har and smell the sweetest flowers,
But I feed not the little flowers; I hear the warbling birds,
But I feed not the warbling birds; they fly and seek their food;
But Thel delights in these no more, because I fade away,
And all shall say, "Without a use this shining woman liv'd,
Or did she only live to be at death the food of worms?"

—William Blake

In contradistinction, the Nepalese guruva, calling though preternatural rites, to kindle electrical stars in the blood, by having contingents of people break apart and drift and regather by telepathy. This, the true arcane, the life above vulcanian zones. It is the orbit where the bodiless is trusted, where the proto-solar living world exists, as a sacred electrical drama, as a codex of fire, as a magical agamas of roses.

—Will Alexander

Contents

Legend, a Tease

There was a reckoning and an expanse. A legend is emblematic in another's poem. Scholar's test of acculturation, or how far willing to reach in realms of Thel. Seize. Cross a spiritual border. Rescue? Love for Thel? Kill for Thel? Change the world for her so she does not resist and finally enter once and for all out of indeterminacy—not exactly afterlife. And come to alleviate gateway for adherents to enter so she sees her own corporeal death out-of-galaxy adventure back at her. How many dimensions is Thel? Her name means "desire." Where is she in us? What is time before birth?

There were several incidents
claimed ears for them:
understand birdsong
gift of augury, of Occult
what are the claims of the dead
but I digress . . .
a strange letter arrived at the office
worldly and otherworldly requests
old lovers
lucid dream interlude
Egyptian friend
migration narrative
hospital telepathy
Ptolemaic astrology
lotus as lily
"held back"?
nocturnal meditations:
kheirourgos, from *kheir,* "hand,"
and *ergon,* "work,"
a manual operation on the patient

an umbilical cord reaches to a vocabulary . . .

Voice's Daughter of a Heart
Yet to Be Born

BOOK 1

Innocence

like dreams of infants

dumb-mute

Citadels Thel Leaves Ringing

Citadels Thel leaves ringing, not knowing what they are. Sounds of glee, celebration, a national holiday, or mourning the deaths of heroes. Not mourning the obscure deaths of heroes slaughtered in their beds only, but out at night on a mission, goggles lit up to scare a prowler a lover a ruined industrialist a terror advocate on a beat or out on the battlefield that is a control room thousands of miles away fighting for our way of life. This is new to Thel: checking out our way of life. Concept of bodiless weapon although she might guess at it. We have time travel. We have symbiogenesis. We have the Yogas of the Bardo. Life did not take over the planet by combat but by networking. But now we have apparatuses to mount a deadly thought on a track to take out a wedding party, to target someone we have never met. If we do meet it will be in the hell of the Slough of Despond, where people did not heed the pleas of children. Neuroscience says help, solve. Solve? *Salve.* Way of life when she who has not been born yet is still on the other side. Cave with child handprints, fingers reach to the other side, thin membrane thrums to a spirit world. Other bastions of power on the wasteland that is our metaphysical foundation, empires of the unborn. We visit a moon of Saturn. We contemplate Mars. We circle asteroids with a strange anticipation. We go interstellar. We like the sound of wormhole. It is magic. Thel without footprint, without trace, desiccated, desolate, nothing around, nugatory. Thel who talks with a worm. Thel a figment in the mind of becoming-in-life, of potential, of not-becoming-yet-in-mind, just got dreamed up, a proposal is Thel's gambit for one who would be cautious. Caution overrides curious. Becoming-curious retreats in the caution mill. Will not engage. Thel becoming angel, though not ministering. Will not turn forward or turn counter-wise. Does not want to burn in the night. But the walls of a discotheque close in, outside her mind, stampede stomps down fragile teen bones. Crunch and twist under the mayhem. Thel is not mayhem. She eschews the nightmares of stampede, of mayhem. Would not go there would not enter. Thel is not empire. Thel is a wisp you trusted but hardly noticed. Brushed from your eye. Swatted away. Small filament in the bright day that gleams. Does one gleam before vanishing? If so, ready.

Thel in prison. Thel without a pencil to her name. But a prophetic ray from the corridor's light to see her by. Almost forgotten: of *Not ready? Not ready yet?* Thel as principle mover in this text of redemption from anterior charnel ground, the place from which all life and death evolves. Thel floats she floats again she floats above vicissitudes, decay, and fecund possibility because unborn. Floats. Thel resolves to play the mummer if we can use that word "resolve." There is no resolve in unbornness. To play dumb-mute when Thel exhausts her questions of quantum futurity. Mummer's play within the poem. Set the stage: Child enters in gauzy costume of quantum futurity before the rough textures set in. Sings lines. Bows, collapsing bodies at the close. Slings of child eyes, arrow, a stone incubating for the heel of day, for terminus. The pit, the grave, images of the shrouded bodies of little children lined up for burial. Brutal world. When will Thel arise, meet her own power? Thel's physique is small, she trembles with the insubstantial leaf. Her actor is similar, mirrors her ancient sister, plays her odd passive panic, quizzical small glimmerlight in eye to ask why, *Why alive? Be alive?* Hell's image is of a glaze you will not see in this life. Perhaps under the sea, illusory aught by a natural-although-filtered light. That light will have traveled centuries to meet a face before its assumption. Faces will tell Thel not always what she needs to know. What need she know? She is ascending. When Thel lifts her head, flowers feel it in their cellular dance. She is like water for them, she is a kind of thirst unsatiated. Her Offworld is womblike, and safe to venture out when the metabolism is not cloaked not clocked. The unborn reaches into her vocabulary to "starry" a sentence that would relieve the others of their woes and cares but because she is not established, no home! No shelter! She does not know her way about, mistakes her standing, her possibility for survival, the postures that she should take with Other, with outside. She considers the limits of human existences that can be crossed briefly within a life. She is tested in this catachresis. Limits. Borderlines. Will outside ever help. In Offworld? You have a fine reticulation, a soft spot or harbor for innocence. When the lights roll Thel will be gone. She will find the semantics to disappear. But first she will manifest her conceptual power. Her androgyny.

A meme of unbornness, a *Philosophia Mundi,* will be from the other side, *in a state of grace before jumping back on the wheel.* Didacters, take note. Detractors, back to your neuroscience labs. Light years away from the hospital station, waiting for news, suited up with gear to avoid the waking living walking dead whose contact might waste you away. The night the friend's heart stopped, those in the car below her apartment heard a knocking on the car, *Wake up, my friends, I am trying to reach you.* She could move through walls. *My poets! I am watching you.* She was everywhere as we cast her ashes in various spots that were entwined with her identity. *I see you,* the ashes sang. We heard her in our minds. Thel back on the other time's side. Back to Offworld. What can she bring back to us? The armored personnel, the doctors and nurses and aid workers and other trainees who risk lives in the interminable plague and triage dynasties. Recognize her light gait. Thel hovering. Shut their hearts on you. Seen too much been too much there done that going to take care of my world move too much farther out move away from this contagion. Leagueless under sea, or in my Offworld conveyor, a belt to the heavens. Thel understands physics without the terminology. She travels, she wears herself out. Poor, nowhere to go.

What is Thel's relation to objects? Can she touch the amalgam become a sorcerer of offers, the accoutrement of animal parts and their attendant powers, Thel be a magician when she decides to enter bodily? What is her mount? Tiger, antelope, lark, serpent, worm? There's an animation of the inorganic in all this writing. She could grab the rattle and shake it. She could restrain the molecules before dissolution. Would she notice mayflies and sing a villanelle?

But wait. The page does not resist, the appendages are those of factotum as she witnesses the ceremonial relief and disappearance of all held dear who may speak with clay and flowers and clouds. Clouds want to hang on (or out) and will only listen up to point of noetic. Know that. Dissolve quickly. Self-dispossession, living corpse, what is my art if not to make us breathe and speak with clouds. Ratchets up the ante on purpose and calling. Take off my mask; I must breathe your tainted air, be one with you. I am written for reason. I am connected to all the things of this world. Painted pebbles out of caves, signs of Paleolithic, human schematizations. Am I ready?

Thel longs for happier climes. The flowers will wilt before her prelude concludes. She will grope for the words that dissolve as sense perceptions fade . . . hold a minute. Thel meanders. Thel considers choice. Then Thel becomes radicalized enough to abort herself. Thel wanted the screens of her investigation to prevent disclosure, as she spied on the intractability of palpable intervention that wouldn't lead to joy. She comes from a tribe of women who do not welcome discord. Joy is wanted. Swerve to it.

In animation the cloud speaks with the voice of a trained actor. Too sonorous, perhaps? Actors make forces of nature speak and garner sympathy. They enter the entr'acte on their own time, mumble mantras of exclusivity, become shepherdesses with crook-wands. Flounce. Gifts of mimetic dancing. And scent of lily gives peace to milking cows. Thel lives with women. Actors as women are the mediums and referees for the force of Nature as they splurge the large screen, paid supplicants perhaps, but they are really behind-screen in the studio with their lines, carefully scripted and rehearsed. They might not even know what they look like as stage presences, as "cloud," as "lily," as "worm," as "clod of clay." They are doing a notable, specific job. But then they would surely watch the animation in a special chamber with possibilities of recording over the pictures for timing and resonance with the image gesture. Hang voices to anthropomorphic cartoons. A cloud has been drawn to resemble a morphed-up version of morphing human (as we speak), which could be a problem for Thel's investigation. Cloud gives shelter, cloud with no identity, cloud shelter does no harm.

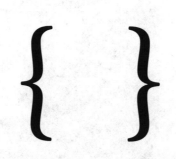

brushed past my own sex

Elucidarium

enter not this elucidarium
not just yet
stay innocent, confused, dreamless?

the cloud is post-historical, the cloud is deracinated, the cloud is the container of all the animals, a serpent is cloud-like in its sway, the sea anemone shares hiddenness with cloud, cloud conceals then reveals, cloud has an upper hand, cloud forgives, then cloud takes ephemera for totality, is cloud male? the cloud is a guide to the humans and is seductive

klutaz, gel, kiode, clot

worm is my puzzlement, when it is infant the worm is dependent on other, on mother, on poetry, when the worm is infant it is vulnerable to the elements and biting things, when the worm is infant it is as fodder it is as nutrient it is the plaything and nourishment for the robin

when the worm is *wurm,* when it is *wyrm,* when it is also serpent and scorpion, it carries the insinuation of sexual prowess, it is the penis, it is arousal, it is also weak of will

leirion, lilie, lis, lirio

when the lily lives it gives purity to the stations of God
when it falters the head bows, hanging lamp of the lily

the clod of clay is trodden with the cattle's feet
it is a scare, it is what we come to, it is sickly and maternal

do we live for others or do we live for ourselves?

if
 daughter
    of desire
 be cautious
      hand reticent
rescinds
mechanical operation,
terror incognita
    if she rears up pincers,
something not so soft,
    if she fades if rained upon
rain itself a disappearing act
disappears
no force or hand to mouth
desperate imitation of power,
    then what is will to
painted doll?
synched—
a will will do
will for self and others

         cinch
assuages
in will
why be willful
   why make query
 if ephemeral things
restrain world's will
in willingness
or adhesion to desire?
trace not wilted?

composite membrane
gravity's objection
to she-without-a-body's metabolism

Dear Locator:
smell the Auvergne
a poetics of ecstasy
template for literary intervention
no more forgetting

    apparatuses:
eyes ears nose hands
 when you don't need them
   progress in linear way
blunt absorption,
  would you recognize
rude traffic, bullish mores
 without a body?

sylvan excitement
  she never entered
she never existed
   she could still be hovering

   lower-right-hand
corner on a square

figures as they disappear
held vertiginous
in verticals, a daughter's
face in lower
quadrant
frame of movie
did that face survive in DNA?

what is it to "fade"?
in movie you see lovers
dissolve or
merge,

that is France
in Egypt you receive dimension

documentaries seethe
Bollywood grips Nepal
in bouncy space
and here, home soil
a constitution dissolves
until bodies ebb
here, the plutonium factory
is mandatory memory
with accoutrements
puts a hand in padded sleeve to
manipulate poison
now remembers to leap back
out the lab door, Exhibit A
don't enter here . . .
it's too "vérité"

outlook to
toxic planet . . . "abandon hope"

prognostication out-sciences
divination
is innocence wisdom?
can't be innocent
   and wise

no perpendicular blood flow
   or change of assemblage
as unborn
      abstract hypnosis notwithstanding,
takes a coat off
      recombinant feathered-rainbow affair
raiment of gods

ça va bien?
 lonesome faraway look
as if frozen in reject-mode
  other side of experience
covert arborescent models,
 analogous potential
process to plan to plan alert to
 plan abort to willpower a *plahn*
    intrude intervene explicate plan
 alert to convert
contexts hand-to-pole or
    prosody's lesson plan
in a taste of the lament
 incorporeal noncapacity

Thel, uneasy rider
 came part way
Thel as inquiry
Thel in elation
Thel close to fading ones
snowflakes on a warm rock
arise and die
writ in truth serum

changes way you relate to reality
inherently perfect, Thel's
consciousness, ignited by impermanence but
cuts obstacles before they arise
hear me, writers, know in future lives,
you are fragile entities
how near to death by tech you are
with your injected substances

Thanatos, Morpheus, Hypnos—all brothers to wee Thel

dimension to understand another
 no-longer-green-system
   as she moves her question forward
Why fade the lotus of the water?

dissolving, I'm fading away, I am going, *sayonara*
the meek shall inherit my cloak of tears *arrivederci*

getting to know the mind no bardo outside the mind
au revoir, I'll be seeing you
no existence *bonne nuit* outside the mind
no awakening outside the mind *ma'a salama*
we go, *zaijian*

self-mind and moment
held together by
 kindness memory renders
    purifying your life
 with time you misplaced

tragic buffo opera
why an ear, a whirlpool fierce
 to draw our creations in?

 propulsive mishap
     rude stick pummels
  awake in leper's tent
blue plastic on walls
orange mesh nets
     hold you in
tin roof leaky in rain
wear down
as you listen

Dear Locator: Buddha teaches that all composite forms are transient, that all conformations are subject to sorrow, that all conformations are lacking a self.

How then can there be Nirvana, O virgins O innocents, how be a state of eternal bliss?

And the Blessed One, breathed forth solemn utterance: There is, O daughters, a state where there is neither earth, nor water, nor heat, nor air; neither infinity of space nor infinity of consciousness, nor nothingness, nor perception nor nonperception; neither this world nor that world, neither sun nor moon. It is the unborn. That O daughters, neither coming nor going nor standing; neither death nor birth. It is without stability, without change; it is the eternal, which never originates and never passes away. There is the end of sorrow.

There is, O daughters, an unborn, unoriginated, uncreated, unformed. Were there not, O daughters, this unborn, unoriginated, uncreated, unformed, there would be no escape from the world of the born, originated, created, formed. Since there is an unborn, unoriginated, uncreated, and unformed, therefore is there an escape from the born, originated, created, formed.

all but the youngest heard the Buddha particles

younger than others, seeking secret air
Voice's Daughter spoke out

"Did you know the inexplicable gait of star?"
"Did you know that someone could inhabit your vision like this?"

doubtful, Thel?

skepticism of young sprite
balks, pulls back attention
horror-splintered
flees toward vales of Har

that systems are available
that angelic guides live within them
that they arise in flocks of innocence

you actualize those with acting jobs?

shuttling actors to their appointed stations?

being in charge being animal
becoming survival acting-in-being
becoming temporary as one-acting-on-in-being
being traveler, one of the desperadoes
schooled in documentary surviving
of scene exchange
helps grok the relative world
its curves and fissures-in-being
its massive exclusivities-in-being
means being held down
for a bacchanal examination

where you suffer detail, poet

a mocking residency
where one breathes the same air you sit in
at a workstation, shape shifting, Thel

neuroscientists doubt that
infants dream
(few emotions, no memories)

their brains are too busy
building neural pathways
developing language
   as birds learn songs
during sleep

Occitan
Obal, din lou limouzi
La-bas dans le limousine

[As far as we got that day in Thel adaptation: a performance of cloud of lily of worm of clod of clay. Our assignment was to assimilate the lesson of Thel with yet again another question: How are you contemporary with your time?]

poetics of ecstasy a possible escape
diamond matrix
don't abandon gone worlds
gaze out on ley lines
planet lives already gone into the earth
read them as a book, a scholarly condensary
dust motes in a dream, speeded-up codex of gone beyond gone

I visit my vision and hear the fossil fuel skeletons jabber
"Oh this was already in the days of the great water"
(refers to Dido, who, abandoned,
sails away in the great ship
while she laments fate and is stopped from
killing herself)

a palinode, and in her famous aria, Dido
stops the world shuddering into her own grave
Thy hand, Belinda . . . when I am laid in earth

falling all over in love again

I brushed past my own sex
twitching body
saw-toothed pattern
vibrates the brain scan

don't enter here?

turn back? or arrive with infant joy?

I reimagined imbalance because it was strife
to communicate this in urgent role
self-appointer, inhabitor, inhibited
kinetics of tragedy, obligatory wasteland,
she-in-me said she had had it with activism
she would go down for tragedy now
she said she had dwelled in the master's house too long
O swore off master his books his poems neat in
exacting margins and containers
and tropes of predictable compliant rage
swore off discomfort in the sacred but affordable notebooks
doom-theorems of universes with unprecedented dangers
greater mishap
Endtime scenario playing out
this was the adult no-nonsense Thel speaking
inside the Elucidarium, testing herself

Thel traveled
wanting thus to be lucky
to be anterior
to be kept dancing
I said guessing to the Voice
who said simply "try it"
make it more movie than stage play
strap on the sex toy
penetrate what you don't know

that this form of projection is ambivalent
and see it work as such

because modest is the daughter-mind

realize it as if sharing / shaping dream: modesty
sips discretion, the appointed masters and little table manners
so one has entered space as indirect transmission
where no thing is real but curiosity
customs fly by, as empty and unfamiliar
as disappearing celluloid

samsara is a handy way to complain:
glittery dark age

whirlwind
or not so unsolvable
rain forest, at risk

where a daughter was a plateau:
a border or vehicle
a description of space

a drama of responsibility
a trenchant objective

Thel means "still," "luminous," "unborn," "empty"
things are apparently real
and the suffering that one experiences of this
is easy to pronounce: *desire*
Blake knew revolution turns both ways

wisdom was likened
he licked it
rim of the golden bowl

a model for offtime world
becoming a new person

sights on liminal willpower
had not developed
baffled, takes rest
unprecedented danger
mere theorem, topsoil
from a SANE blast 1957
much lost, *inestimable*

and would oppose all conflict
(Martin Luther King Jr. enters here)
undo in jump-drive speed our nuclear "choice"?

that was a policy, remember the MX and Pershings?
missiles, haunting sleep, we protest

need some oneirogens here
take the edge off
and lucidly sleep
meet the guide in a dream
stop the bomb in a dream

Cartesian doubt cannot bind you!

love the body the lover said, and lover's pheromones
come hither to the Elucidarium
where we explore the obscurity of various things:
antichrist, purgatory, last judgment, temptress Magdalene,
like a razor of circumstance
a sharp guise as thy tiny anthem faces

and come inside the seductive connectome
the brain's permanent record of intelligence,

where memories, meanings emerge from orgasmic links
epigenetic rustlings
every thought every sensation
tiny electrical impulses make their way

that we still exist as voice
and talk back with nature
that we are an extension of nature
but lost our way
killed our own reward
and forgot to speak when nature needed us most

The girl-child Kumari goddesses are incarnations of Taleju or Durga. They live in temples and are carried in chariots during festivals and worshipped by thousands.

A symbolic "fire eye" is printed on their foreheads, and they only wear red.

They go through several goddess tests including spending the night among the heads of ritually slaughtered goats and buffalo. They retire upon puberty.

"I could not walk properly because I had been carried all the time. The outside world was a stranger to me, but as goddess I played my part very well."

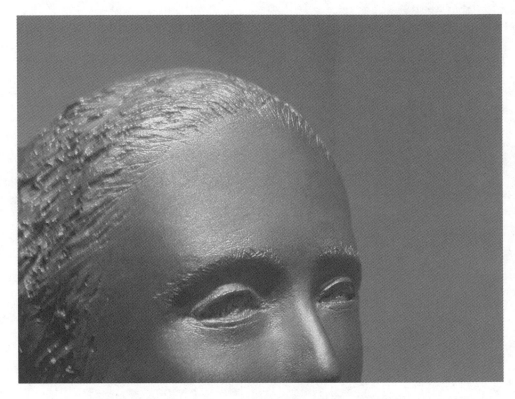

to come into light, lily

Dear Locator

It was in the deep of summer that the letter arrived, addressed to the "Disembodied Poetics Locator" and asking the whereabouts of its director. I had appeared in the writer's dream informing him of a teacher residing in Autun, France. He wanted to travel there. What kind of teacher, I wondered—spiritual? educational? Rosicrucian? in the fields of poetry or performance or as we now say "hybrid" creative work? His was a hybrid dream. I had published a book entitled *Helping the Dreamer* some years back. Self-fulfilling prophecy? Could I be of help?

The madcap writer of the letter wanted further information on how to locate this apparitional teacher from me. In fact he requested that the Disembodied Poetics Office send any information it might have that would further assist him in his quest. He also indicated we had had a cup of tea together once some years back in Sundance Square, a café in Fort Worth, Texas. I had little recollection of this, yet it seemed a grounding and personal detail and assured me that the writer had actually had me in his dream, and not some other public figure he wanted to loop into his mania. I found myself searching my own recent dreams, wondering perhaps if we had crossed wires or psychic paths. I recalled a recurring dream within which a spiritual teacher, now deceased, a reincarnated lama in the Buddhist tradition, a generous man of great reputation, appeared to me, often instructing me and others on how to live underground when the *dark ages, and they are coming, my friends, coming soon* would arrive and threaten our very existence, depriving us specifically of all the teachings we held dear—spiritual and literary practices from many wisdom traditions: gnostic, Sufi, indigenous, Taoist, Celtic, Shinto, Diné, Cargo, Uralic, Rasta, Druze, et cetera, as well as tomes of poetry, literature, philosophy (in many marvelous tongues) and I remember here a question about music, and how we would all need silencer microchips so that we might, in our hidden dwellings below, stay quiet, not bring attention to our vibrational presence and in our role as guardians, protectors of "the realms" as our lama called us to be. We would not be able to move our bodies, sway or turn or stomp the ground in ecstasy, with the music that was unheard in any case in public space. Rather we would evolve a coded internal dance pulse or rhythm known solely to us. We would be able to hook up together as the wizards of the upper Amazon did in their collective visions. We would live likes moles in subterranean caverns without ritual implements or instruments. No flutes! No drums! Abandon our animal cries and monkey howl, bellow of elephant, her pang her pain. We were now designated as illuminati, Templars, holders, elders, trance-adepts, seers, progenitors, and the like. As with the magic practices of the Lacandon Jungle we would all imbibe the same vision. This was in my repeating dream, as I have said, but this thought bubble more like an afterlife vision let me call it that as the palpability of the tall looming figure giving transmission gave my life responsibility and purpose and a sense of urgency. I tried to hone skills adept in the practices of preservation. I often imagined persons-of-the-future being dismayed at how little remained of the civilizations in front of them. What knowledge and guides to the scintillating questions had been lost, just as space exploration devices went off course and crashed and exploded in remote places, all that data compromised or as memory waned, how little the curious ones—those coming after—would reclaim knowledge. Know how to dance a polka, even, a tarantella. What was a masque? How are you wired? Why did you ever want to know anything? And the ensaladas of Sor Juana? What was a neuron? An expurgated black box to explain all loss. It would enter the trauma of the Anthropocene, margin of many causes.

Ground zero, familiar trope. Razing of countless cities. Gaza, Erbil, Tikrit. Aleppo, Homs, al-Bukamal, Deir al-Zour, shifting sands, Alexandria, still standing? local tribal control, contested: border posts, Kurd-held, maps of pain. Thousands in the camps, under ruby sky.

The recent destruction of the eighth-century citadel of Assyrian king Sargon II at Khorsabad. Nimrud destroyed, March 2015, CE.

Once, when in an induced coma under surgeon's blade, I encountered the specter of one of my dearest friends, an adept of biological spheres who could analyze glacial and animal majesties into their scientific components, setting coordinates of the multiverse to the rings of time in every redwood tree. As he departed this world as he passed as he went to the great homecoming, night of a full moon in April, he swerved toward me, and we brushed arms in the bardo. We touched consciousness (I felt—how to describe?—his "tone"?) but coming back "to," urgent and still undead, he turned away fleeing down another well-lit corridor. Awake in the relative world he had already departed the Chiricahua Apache charnel ground, close to the now no-longer extinct jaguar corridor, leaving behind a multirayed native blanket in a bed of flowers.

Just a bit longer, I begged of no one in particular because my traditions and practices were nontheistic. I was talking to myself. *Extend this life . . .*

My assistant was amused yet wanted to get on with the business at hand (evaluations and requests and obligatory recommendations for positions of poetry in workaday mode) and seized the note, tossing it perfunctorily into the wastebasket where I promptly retrieved it, seeing it as possibly useful and revelatory. I needed a luminous detail. A trigger. A rune, a conundrum, a paradox, I needed to keep writing *to live* if nothing else a way into further dream work that was starting to investigate various yogas and preparation for life-after-death states. The Yogas of Naropa.

Wanting to put my assistant's mind to rest that I was not drifting into a world of mindless Occult meander, I resisted going on with some morbid patter about death-dream-yoga and the like, or why I might want to retain the message from this kook or what I found intriguing in his note, and told her of the nut file I had kept for years. That was the cynic's response to protect my poet's excitement on the scent of a new adventure. I had trouble staying seated at my workstation, mind on fire.

There was a letter from the fellow with the same last name as mine, who claimed we might already be related and why would I not consider a marriage offer from him now in this new century. He owned a drugstore in Los Angeles and had all the drugs in the world at his reach and my disposal. *Elixirs to counter any troublesome mood swing.* To sweeten the proposal he also offered his luxurious home by the water in Malibu where I could rest weary limbs, with saunas and steam rooms, interior and outdoor pools, and a limousine with chauffeur who could recite poetry to "carry me with the greatest poetic ease" on shopping trips or work engagements up and down the coast. Marijuana was also becoming legalized, he assured me; I could smoke freely in the car, which also had a full bar with marvelous health drinks. Including booster shots, and "Catch a Fire" with beets and cayenne pepper and "Body Good" with Swiss chard and ginger, "just to name a few." This letter was in the file and I did reply in some offhand fashion with regrets and a signed edition of a recent book. I never heard from him again.

There was also a more recent letter from an individual who had proof that Jim Morrison of twentieth-century poet-rock renown was still alive and walking among us and had taken up residency in our town and was enrolled in fact at the school where I worked. I had seen his grave site at Pére Lachaise. Surely Jim was well underground with the worms by now. The letter writer appeared to be in a time warp as Morrison would already be close to eighty years old, hardly a candidate for university education, although nothing is inconceivable and we have had late-education students enroll from time to time. Jim was shy, the letter indicated, and would do nothing himself to expose his true identity, and we were not requested to do anything either, just be aware that this mighty figure, this superstar, the Lizard King, King of Orgasmic Rock, a hallowed art-saint *poète maudit* was still embodied. I paid homage to his Sufi Eagle Dance. From the tone of the letter, the writer did not seem to be aware of any passage of time. Jim was still youthful, had faked his death, and was already embarked on an academic path of accreditation and degree conference. Why would he need a poetry school anyway? He was well versed in Rimbaud, Artaud, Céline, Kerouac.

The file contained other sundry bits of adulation, complaint, plea, and requests of myself to send articles of intimacy. Sorry to rave on about the nut file but a letter from one woman in particular touched me. The sender also spoke of being "unborn" or "not born yet" and certainly hadn't found her voice ("I need to find my own voice!") and of how my example of activism in the realms of poetry would help her make a decision to enter the "strange" life. The double variegated choiceless path of poet. She also said she had encountered me in various ways and although her heart had been hardened against me out of envy and something positive I had said about William Carlos Williams once (she was a feminist), I was back in her good graces now, as she had learned to accept William Carlos Williams as an ally. She had always been wary of doctors. She apologized for any negative feelings ("I have been wrong about you and William Carlos Williams, please forgive me"). She had also had a "medical poetry" dream, a sure indicator of the fixation she now felt toward a feminine role model and groundlessness, of being confused and wanting an elixir as in "Poetry is my medicine, poetry is the cure." I sent her a grounded catalogue full of the particulars of a rooted poetics. But in her dream I was "in the matrix, a large stone." She recounted we were in the state capital. She could make out certain landmarks, "the needle, the Lincoln." We were suddenly being strafed by mandible drones and escaped through a manhole to an underground tunnel like in World War II London. Remember Hilda Doolittle, she said. I then handed her a woven cloth from Nepal, she said (how would this complete stranger know I had such a cloth?—still have it now, much faded after forty years from that first trip to the Kali Temple. A complex weave. She sensed I was also (and I am sure I was, but in some other direction) not yet fully active in all the things of this world. Crisscross dream more prevalent in these days in the things of this world, in the Great Reckoning.

There were also missives recounting religious fixations. A boy who had escaped from a Xtian Satanic cult (his parents) indulging in horrendous "snuff" practices but was now in a fiction cult. (Spelled "fixtian.") Inductees worked on rewriting their lives. True memoir, actual fact, was verboten. Then there was a boy on the front lines of the war in Iraq, angry that not enough of the beatniks had served in the military. He was writing from a foxhole in the middle of the desert. This was the first Gulf War. God was not happy about this, he said. Sleep of reason producing monsters. You know someone said that. "Men who meant to be wild," he said, "should first serve." I thought this was a semiprofound statement, I mean about serving. On second thought it's Puritan boytalk.

The punk daughter of Mormon faith who was enamored of "William Blake the Antinomian," as she referred to him, wrote to us initially, but actually visited our classrooms and had a band by similar name, "Blake & the Antinomians," in a nearby local town. She was at odds with her family because she was a Blake-loving Mormon. "We need to stick together," as one of the Quorum of the Twelve said, scolding her and with scorn, as she recounted to me. Then what he said was, "Blake had his own system; we have ours." I was curious and a bit uneasy that the Quorum knew about William Blake, mistrusted him, and might use this against this delicate child of punk. What else did they have their eye on? The Muggletonians were certainly not in their book of prophecy.

Mostafa, my companion of Egypt days and our romantic time in the desert, would often write to this address, my workstation, sending poems but also plaintive requests. "I am still undocumented. Maybe you can help me get to the west to our campfire conversation." He was in the middle of a revolution. This was not archival material for amusement; I genuinely cared for him, but his letter sat alongside the appeal for help from the poet in Juárez with death threats at her door. This was the time of the horrible murders of young women from the maquiladoras. And our own country's huge social unrest. To make the case for citizenship, we would work on that, write memos to the lawyer, letters of support.
Mostafa, hear me, you too, I will not abandon . . .

This was the time of frequent immigration . . .

I thought about serving. Does worm serve? Cloud serve? Lily and clod of clay? Serving is a rollercoaster in that it may never end. Whom to serve, what ethos, what philosophos, what do you value, believe in, are passionate about, whom to please? What do you put your life to, tithe your time to? Serving with alacrity's vow to stay busy. Or let them walk over you. Is serving ever easy surrogate magic? May you serve poetry, old taskmaster? You could never serve enough because at every angle you are serving microbes and they are endless. We were serving in our edifice, our evanescing office, with black mold growing under our daily bread.

There had been the flood, now categorized as "incident." We were under-paid cultural workers. *That was a lame joke about bread,* Andrea said.

Often communications of sympathy came in for the difficult weather we were enduring as we tried to maintain our academy, our alchemy. Floods had come and gone and *may be back,* one shaman from the Candomblé tradition (a dance in honor of the gods) remarked. More blue water. You would serve weather if you understood it "in the name of Ezekiel" said another-who-hears-the-voice and sees the writing on the walls and so on. In some traditions it is a female voice, this voice of God. Or God's daughter rising through the Kabbalah. Presumably one is caught off guard as one hears the dulcet voice of God through the female. You might mishear. Fires pandemic in these parts. The flood (*move to higher ground*) had washed away homes of close associates. The color blue was an important medi-tation. We had driven around seeing huge fissures in the earth. Gigantic rocks had been moved. Promethean tasks. Whole topographies shifting. You wonder about the call to being human. Were people rethinking their progeny? *Born in this world, you've got to suffer . . . shift a load to the Lord . . .* and so on.

Endtime prophets were getting to be a bore for some of the community. With their Endtime pamphlets (who hands out pamphlets anymore?). Although many noticed the hail was growing larger and more frequent and more important to itself. Egoistic aggressive hail. Tornados were seen descending from the sky. This was the nut file in a nutshell.
But there was more to come.

and then . . .

blurts out about hail as if omen.
and then one went in a car to seek shelter.
another accident.

people in vehicles in intermediate years.
constantly at risk.

wait for the new light-rail bullet transport we'd voted for.
promises of politicians along with amendments on
personhood.
a retro automobile hood is all we get.
behemoth, scourge of the environment.
and hit again, warning will we please listen.
Endtime: twisters, bodies cryogenized.
the time I was offered a hand
and a place to sit in a motel in Ann Arbor
next to the not-as-yet-murdered British rock star.
flowers for him, flowers for his tomb.
others live on in semiretirement.
I wanted to be a Locator for all my thoughts, help me
sundries of the collectome.
bring all the bluesmen and dead rock stars back too.
get them to found some schools for poetry.

one rock star walking among us.
we would check the attendance sheets.

do rock stars ever die? the child asks.
did not want to die, I explain.
kept singing in ragged voices
till the cows come home.
influence on men.
like Calvinist idealism.
and dysnomia.

Dear Locator
be efficacious.
be remembered.
you are called by the wrong name.
chattel, bound feet, slave girl.
don't take that lightly.
over which elite guardians preside.
walk like an Egyptian.

could be woman you seek or child.
ask mole who burrows under.

are you morphing identity
  to keep stride with dark time
capital sucking your cock?

a French revolution.
helping the dreamer, America.

thunderous sound.
old mole? old mole?
do poets ever die?
never.
they never want to die
except at end of the poem.
time out before tsunami
explained it like the
Dinanukht
Mandaean demon from the marshes
of southern Iraq
who sits by the waters
between worlds,
writing himself
half man, half book
writing as he reads.
a life sentence.
his hand under his own binding,
his shroud, his turban
writing . . . or like the rabbit scribe
of the potent Mayans
or Thel, her own book
already written
or hail the size of image
transference.

spectacle for Endtime.
still writing ourselves
  in eloquence too.

size of fear, waiting sentence.

and intervention on any sentence's death knell.

children worry.
about being enshrouded.
engulfed, ensouled.
while they are stuck in aporia.
unaware how fear moves their elders.
lily an adult.
cloud explicitly male.
clod what color.
mysterious voices
in clod realm masking
transmission. about
death, about existence.
children wait repair.
dream a way out of empire.
undertaker's paradise.
stacking the graves.
children go mute.

lily whose lotus self
is Neoplatonic shadow.
animal realm synesthesia.
realm of Paracelsus.
Jakob Böhme.
Antinomian long enough
to come into light, lily.
come from alienation.
come to light, lily.

lily is a system
come from alimentation,
    come now.

hear voices.
lily lily.
infant lily.
sing now.
 walk in garden.
   come to light.
lily, infant lily
never limp in limitation
never lapse
lingo
lily, come, come to light
in dilemma's use.
amuse.

easternmost extent
of Umayyad campaign
stops here for
idols in small boxes.
destroys them.
what if these
symbols exist simultaneously
with our schema?
become human, atavistic.
what if Albigensian prophecy
releases a soul from human coma?
what if consciousness, soul,
whatever instance,
life-becoming-flesh-in-transit
    returns
does harm?
out of the box

into the garden?
these were questions for Endtime.
trays of divinatory offerings
in a school of
rhetoric eschewing mystery
yet confused.

please advise. still innocent?

do not enter here . . .

Dear Locator,
scrambled.
the desert is a rhizome. you get used to it.
there was an incident involving
daughter-trauma apparitions.
a lover held me.

read ransom note in shaky hand:

THE PIT NOT RADICALIZED

ASTONISHMENT OF EROS IF YOU MAKE MESS

BE REVOLUTIONARY FERVOR

ASTRIDE JOKINESS, OLD MOLE

look into doom.
future is divination.
Thel's riddle getting closer,
she is held in ransom for her next life
which is still perpetual affect.

another memo: "unborn" was challenge. unborn dream, unborn text.
another chance? jury on "afterlife" out a long time. I was the old mole
burrowing into the past and future of a telepathic poetics. to meet a
daughter in outer space an eagle eye could not see meek child.

excessive rain. what was the evacuation plan?

to the one who dreamt a teacher in Autun: *message delivered. and working*
   on it . . .
assure you
another telepathy assignment
walketh in the garden in the evening time
it's very pure air here

Andrea was amused and we went about our tasks—more circumspectly—
for the day.

cthonic phase, more featherly light

Vox Dei

Malibu?
(Chumash: *Humaliwo*)

a birth coil

listening to the voices of the ground
was what I heard the rebbe say
this was today's clue: filament of sound
in ritual astonishment, indigenous

at nightfall reinsert the plugged-in voice
it collapses in private property
enclave of guilt and fear, then escapes
to the parting of the Red Sea,
Sea of Reeds

in Judaism and Christianity the *bat kol* or *bath ḳōl,*
the daughter of a voice, is a heavenly voice that proclaims God's judgment

it is said that the sound comes from an invisible source

ye heard voice of words and saw no similitude, no book saw no book
    heard none but the
oral in the head, bat kol a wondrous but small thing
the rebbe consulted said, "yea, it is a small thing":

only heard a voice of one that spake words, no book, saw none

a still, small voice saying "Elijah, Elijah"
a revelation, a hum, caused by motion of all things
that fill the whole world
    as a voice comes out of a cloud . . .

from heights from warring Jerusalem from Gaza
from thunder
from roar of the sea
heard small condensation on rock arousing itself
heard moth wing move, heard lament of gull

falling from heaven,
heard cry of stricken mother for her fallen,
as through tears
fallen children, the voice said
wash the world with tears

Nebuchadnezzar to thee it is spoken
kingdom is departed from thee,
kingdom is but a small voice to thee

hand of God, which is voice of waves
signifying echolocation of all spheres
nature as a projection into a human that needs
to project back at you

nature is us talking back to ourselves,

"we are your nature," lamb bleats

Arabs tell of a voice—*hâtif*—that calls to
lost travelers in wilderness
and the *munadi* came in solitude of night
to poet Nizami when he despaired

Ezekiel hears voice's daughter,
murmuring like a dove
he hitches her poem
to future stars' embryology

sobers
small muscles
thrills metabolism
says look that soft blue form,
voice like smoke

true bat kol goes mad in human time
reminder in human time of vocables trying to reach us
in human time, no doubt but debt in human time
bat kol only heard how humanity
stopped the next dimension
(voices will travel)
and you might step on a twig and out of that
sound arises, which is daughter of God's voice
word and emotions saying *here, you are here*
larynx in the making
be everywhere, daughter who vexes night

dochter, dhuktar, dohtar, dottir, Tochter, daughter, dhugheter, duhitar,
dugeda, dustr, dust, dukt, thygater, filia is feminine of filios . . .
daughter-who-vexes-night.

come to judgment, daughter-who-vexes-night
lurk here at womb mouth

see the seduction of innocence

Thel with broken cloud-wings
(she who sleeps on a swan's wing)
tympanum of last tagged judgment
fragged before her time
sometimes the shout of a nation
it's nation time at womb mouth

in Tibet a medium speaks in a notion of
lhabab, god-descending,
or *lha bka',* god-speech
she, oracle, *mo-ma, pamo,*
bard-medium, narrates epics
transcends social liminality
otherwise laypeople go about
ordinary lives (victims of cultural / religious genocide)

Celtic Aedui
and cult of Mary the Magdalene
come inside echolocation's
holy radar, do not cast a stone

born at rainbow crest
and still walk a curve at Endtime
but what coordinates come together
matrix of doom? part your seas
how far will Thel travel in your eukaryotic vision?

three Marys journey to Autun
gesture their sanctity
suckle and go on
feel cobblestones under feet's martyrdom
is she a guide, mourning dove?
did Thel live with you long, cut up a grasping mind?
enter trenches of feminine guile and its vocabulary?
locked within walls of stony calyxes
never virgin birth
but sprung from a poet's inner eye, a fourth moment?

chrysalis gestates auguries
   within a conch shell
stone eggs

emerge from inside gourds,
glistening melons
hold cradles within a tomb
chaotic voices in warning mode
before entering the grove
Old English *grat*—
grove, copse,
akin to *graeta*—thicket
from proto-Germanic *Graef*—grave, ditch
Old Norse *gróf*—cave
brim site on a river bank
birth bed, death bed?

perhaps a protective syllable lowers
into the woman through the
top of her head
and becomes the waist of the child
syllable "V," a drop of sesame oil
on the tail of a deer at the beginning of time
what else goes into first human being?

this book connects to the navel of
a transmigrating woman yet to come

place a gem in mouth of her corpse
for the next cycle

   in dulcimer space, new woman, sex unnameable

these beings before they take birth have miraculous abilities
walk on water   see with divine eyes   never age
and vocalize

formation of eyes in the embryo
evolve with sounds in the womb
and expand with explosions from outside
eye-like features called "the eye of the lamps" appear
Locator is *axis mundi*

tell me everything you know about birdsong and poetry!

standing in recovery
a theogony
reading all the books in the world

fine Egyptian glaze to Thel's expression
hieratic faience

child come close
sprite, all lit up, attentive
antennae on fire

otherwise in a time of entertainment
we begin to lose our minds
as predators kill to survive

wandering minds ask
what is reality
where can I rest?
where can I take birth?
who will love me?

it's a dark room
devoid of color
human body will be created again when it is
nothing but bones and dust

body waiting for its orders
become bronze
"All in timing"
(a feather brushes your thigh)

love is cyberconnective
chthonic phases, more feathery light
tension of the heart
mind is moist

why not free on little bed of desire?

see through you to older side:
resembles a forest
see through you to the other side:
resembles timber bower
resembles rainbow of eccentric color
emanating from industrial waste
our squat, nihilistic punk days
full of glory and burnout
a measure of sound, making love

would enter here? on command?
ray emanating from a child's scalp
carved with "V" for Victory
what is that raw color . . . of blood

       not here, would not enter here, russet

what is the spectrum of child's pain

no, not enter there

(seduce me, I might be persuaded)
what comes in here to disappear?
get rid of person; all of you
tie up your heart in a squatter's cell

get rid of your pronoun once and for all
troubled to centuries, refugee identity

motor is arms
arms are as motor fronds
what are they saying your neck of a woods?
what do they whisper?
lift & lift
lilt & lilt & lift to lilt
   not enter here
mere appropriation
lesser motility
moving millions of bodies in diaspora

yet dawn brings warmth
voice brings warmth

sound debate
rings, Thel on a pedestal

you might desire to know your ideas better
as maimed statuary
or as scorpion who masks her sting

as brooch altered your eye
or oddity of scarf
what was embedded in the gypsy camp?

what kind of orgiastic medicine in the future?

ability to grow back limbs,
ability to grow back breast et cetera
or become a man, tested by testosterone
but nongendered, vehicle for greater power

twisting inside inner ear
am not your kind of century or beauty
universe hits with toxicity

prompts of little use, am not

flash of a spirit went by, *vox dei*
sprung of mother's knee

primary art shows red on the outer part
violet on the inner side caused by light
refracted when entering a droplet of water
rest in there, inchoate womb

non-dual primordial energy
stands astute in
"there was an incident"
or love affair
the New World calling
sexes separated out
mystical phantom market
as if a deity arrives to distribute largesse
call it "property," "land"
North America: her little plot of clay

wheel run down on Offworld
someone said "sabotage"
Locator working overtime
voices insistent on this: be rational

we made tea in the gypsy camp
tell more stories, he begged
about your deities, your *vox dei*
America's doom and promise
how it slaughters its innocents
visions, past lives
everyone a nomad
out here by the Red Sea
Mostafa handed me the tin cup
too hot to hold

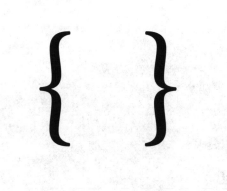

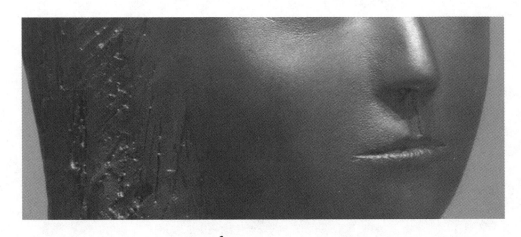

forgetting where the moon was putting herself

Urn Singer

come out
    of amnesia's cloud
join the urn singer who turns on a gyre

singing of written bodies not food of worms
    dream bodies   spinning
    finally protest bodies emerge from the documentary she narrates

"What you noticed is young women occupying the street, the site, the library, with defiance. A whole environment fierce in alternative, defiant. OCCUPY you must. *Our streets.* And the speed at which something is devoured, spits back up although the ethos never changed will teach you how to live in dilemma. We are still a debt culture, but we go underground, let the fickle-of-heart who steal and undermine the OCCUPY meme crash and burn."

Tahrir still in the urn.

All sites of rite and protest intersect, converge in urn: cave we meet in to plot our revolution, Wall Street, Times Square, Union Square, Brooklyn Bridge, Harlem, Maidan
Performing in a trance of nonbecoming but to be Mostafa's Egypt dimmed by nonbeing, Thel weeps.
She embodies *anutpāda:* having no origin, not coming into existence,
    underlying emptiness
quantum sphere of the not-born-yet activist who haunts the marketplace where broken shards disarm the dreamer

Urn singers mount the rim of jar and proclaim their vision.
Inhabit the nightmare. Liberate the nightmare.

Wary to proceed. Way to proceed. Advanced adversarial flashlights shared with other visitors to nascent Offworld, those who are cogent, immigrants, animal mistresses, border-creepers, sundry troopers, and frequent rabbit rescuers. Consider this a holiday package designed by future tourist guardians. And benefits besides in transference, rehabilitation. Mordant proclivities inherited from the colonies. Once in a time they are standing around a large compass and holding its forcefield. But on the other side of dimension, sensitivities have difficult other compasses at the ready. They read the subtle body with impunity. Adversed. Encompassed as a shadow-field might. Tell you where to put your body on the line, dial tremors, the hand that points to the cardinal pouting, bronze girl scout at the ready. I want . . . *there.* A series of missteps to go into or future masterful arrangements. Thel might not be quite adolescent, nonbody reticence to bleed, that would be anathema to Thel.

Thoroughly attuned nights. Vestals. Way beyond childhood. Gestures indicate desire and not waste time. Identify yourself. *I am dithyramb!* they shout, back from the dead, power in a chorus: WE WANT . . . WHAT'S *THERE. AND TO SHED INNOCENCE. OCCUPY!*

What occurs around the perimeter of migrants is uncommon weather, unfathomable suffering. There is activity, as you might expect, in a small depleted village. But also paranoia of factions, carnage, rooted religious neighbor snitching on neighbor, a totalitarian wind blowing from the east. Not enough supplies, airdrops that make no sense. Gray weather is a different province. Yellow weather is not such a good sign or sure. But noxious. A chemical will root you out. It will emit mastodons or rumor so you'd better prepare. Core mastodon belief structure is wanting. Is the coast clear? Out of the cult chambers. Dragons breathe here. Mastodons seem to relate to the equinox, as do elephants. Elephants had hoped to save us. *Namaste.* Not stardom but peeling of skin, sisters, passing a skull around, caressing it with sinewy trunks. Temperature here is exceptional. Some will avoid injury and thrive, a place of restitution. Gather in field, daughters, to confound becoming-human:

Hatti who loves caves, who sings in caves

Ahhiyawa, an archer of the Future Feminist clan

Lefkandi, Greek agitator, in crisis

Luwian another city dweller, eastern Caucasus

Nydian writes her way out of grief

Elateia wishes to travel with the consciousness of silent things

Hibiscus aspires to take birth in a coil of future feminism

Satella, dancer of radiant tribe

Tekke, who knows how to work the machines

Ambromartyr, tough hybrid sprite

Terrifa, seer and asexual

Anodyne measures herself with healing antidotes

qualities are fixed like epithets

are they chosen?

memories of the virgins from the vales are faint

William Blake did not tell us their names

But only of Thel, a not-stream enterer, the thirteenth fairy, wandering sister. A place of restitution in her demeanor but you may be fooled. She cannot carry us. Although she turns us to ourselves in a self-help way. Is life cheap? Is that the question?

Offworld women smile. Lift the load for greater good. A better form of governance. Temples that make sense, not monolithic eyesores. Chariots and practical urns. Be an urn singer. A place for trees will be set out as you perform. Strive to circle and resist. A place to bury, as you wish, whatever your fancy your praxis your superstition your folly your lineage your dynasty your parentage requires. May it be ritualistic. Utopians of the future: get your grave plot now, good for growing herbs. Tend your ground. A soundless utopia, the phones are silenced in their little beds. Cradles or tombs. Left the new world back to your arms.

Hatti patiently waits with her singing bowls. Circular motifs. Migrant sisters with their plots, planning psychic takeover. A site that indicates global rising.

Magdalene's myrrh bearers thanked the patronage of apothecaries for
    obeisance
thanked the glove makers, the perfumeries, the prostitutes—over 201
    in number—
and tanners and the like for their service
unapologetic *apostola apostolorum*
or women of the "alabaster jar" were not excommunicated as they once
    had been
even though they applied unguents to perfume the flesh in forbidden acts,
fearless in the ruby night

Thel was pale. If things did not grow and die and change we would be stuck in the frame of her eternal dream. How much fun in sighing all the day. A dove's voice mournful, a lily happy to be rayed in light, a little thing she's down for, caught in a silver shrine. Worms at the end of each day. Weary of their toil. But who will find her place in this realm of perpetual displacement? Silver too disintegrates and dies.

Why not pass away, cloud, to love and peace and raptures holy and unreasonable, strange weather and a journey again of finding a wise leader. We will answer in due time. Rock out of their cradles perhaps, drop down here on planet and believe you. Respond to your inquisitors who work your question. Hook in, hook up. Work on it. A meek cloud over Blake's Albion. Wake up, Thel, come occupy.

Compass advocates a kind of mapping still matter-bound, hold awhile and sometimes the interpreter balks. Not a fairy tale but talking about whole communities of resistance. Literary too, ask about the home they live in, unspeakable poverty. Those who rise from dystopia. Why gather around a compass if you are not awry. Why not come to the aid of, why not now compassion. A compass trembles. Have this heart at ready. Occupants of samsara, phenomenal world. Paranormal. All surviving like the delicious elves and fairies in Tír na nÓg. A land of youth. Hidden hills. A meteorological metallurgist seeks out, preys on the fairies' fear of iron. One who makes wheels and fixes treadmills. Conjures wind machines. Camaraderie to an echolocator, who finds things, dangerous, tracking echoes. Menace to the wee ones. Redefines polar attractions. Fairies inhabit interstices. Angels in the ozone. Parts company. Mutterghost. Fix a treadmill. Startle and resist, the executing of wind. Freshens some of our debts. Offworld confirms and appreciates the history of all things relevant to human accomplishment and explanation. Confirms lovers. Without debts, what records? Would not be here without you. In Spanish "to keep legal." José Martí, Gabriela Mistral, Ruebén Darío, Ernesto Cardenal of revolution claim prophecy could not agree more, navigating arts in childhood in poetry. Everything a scramble, mostly hardscrabble. Long time to consider. Future equinoxes. Forgetting where the moon was putting herself, and in relation to her planets, furtively bringing together in an encompassing charity. A special part of the forest will still be a tremble to some of our sisters. To others make folly and a more peaceful talking down objectified as for the baby seals. Robots for our suffering, but isn't empathy a good thing? It will be correct. A section of philosopher's argument was what we had in mind, math wizardry that has its own belief system outside our world. Will propagate. Will join. Will be in ranks of lost empires. Brought to knees. Math couldn't save us. Who measured this?

WHO MADE THIS CITADEL? I DID. BUT IF YOU FUCK WITH THIS, MY REMNANTS, YOU WILL BE DUST.
Whose message breaks off here . . . arrogance, patriarchy.
Resembling the egoproclamation cuneiform of so-long-ago Nimrud's rulers. Citadel gone to ruin.
How did the word get out? And out of hand, gone down under its pillagers. Did you just happen to walk by this pillar of amendment?
And see the sign NOT ENTER HERE? Private property, tear it down!

Contributing a table to a longhouse, filled with little wheels and ducts and trays and receiving accoutrements. Receptacle for true money and symbolic money. A special part of the forest where witches gather. Born of mastectomy. Amazonian in proclivity. We came here surviving the "marks," the "enhancement days" and drugs, the stencils and amputee reconstruction therapies. Metal workers and plastic workers stand together. Medicine is advancing on you. Kill or cure. Stack it up for the warriors, community wants its book written, the long demise ahead of all this. All this? What. Is documented. In a black hole.

Apocalypse, what's all this preparation? Your belief system shreds mine, was a message. Some tussle or fair use. Your belief system kills mine. For the writing bodies this is a problem. Charity only visible in hindsight. As dust settles. Mephistopheles says he saw this once and coming. By chance hunting and gathering edible moss. A pact with his own medicine. He ate and dreamt in an alarm. Called in by the curiosity of a possibility. Milked by prophecy. Eternal life. Who would give it you, who leads. Going to flames. An infant martyr?

Already a gathering, a circle of animals mounted by mystical maidens. Why should any clan get abused of notions that abound the gathering. Beware. Were exceptions to how they organize tributes. A consciousness is thinking it over, about entering this worldly realm. Offworld has a solution in prajna power. A race of diminutive little people and their animal attendants driven into hiding by larger invading humans, needs rescue.

Seed the new enhancement colonies? Stay in aporia, abeyance, zoned-out mortal waiting stations, wait your chance to liberate sentient beings. Toss a limb around while you dally, biding time on the charnel ground, the place where life meets death in twilights of mind. Don't go so dark on me, looking for family connections. Forcing of match-making resumes its odd frequency and forgery. Tangling the hair of sleepers into elflocks is not the only solution. Wear secret clothes inside your own. Dye them green or weave them of living grass. Save water.

Projections in Endtime: Resume your touch, your sense perception of prophecy. How that is examined, explained. Save more water. A child there too, dousing for water. Could be you, waking, waiting for your Locator. To sit around this ephemeral wait station until dawn. An oil drum for light but you see with many eyes as the puppeteer chants parts for the shadows of ghost worlds. One a strong current, feel the others? Of different figuration from yourself. Find your way to your rest station. Out of bounds for martyred, church or temple or shrine. Recompense some of the insurgents, at first reluctant to go there, across a divide. Trace back a history of fleeing persecution, find and found your poetry in a safer land.

Explicitly prying the time machine to activate its mystery again. What is Occult to a machine. It is a cylinder of alphabets, it is a sway of geese treads, it is footprints of every extant and extinct thing. It is fossils, it is memory and rune. It is challenge. It holds mind and indication, it is a swift summation, it is current and not so current, it resides in your breast pocket. It locks you up when you need shelter. It is resilient. Occult is metabolic. It was formed of all children too. To sit around a clearing to make an Offworld, into dawn, into performance. Occult was banned, Occult held hostage, many celebrities of Occult. It is a kind of entrance morphed into a miniseries, into a chamber, into sanctuary, a place tamed the augury, it is a state of mind, it is a dabbling, it is a mystery, it is a hierarchy, it is a respite, it is full of shenanigans, it holds our attention, it is presumptuous, it is accosted with turbans and large rings, it is outside established religious cultures, it is a reaction, it is Antinomian, it is recursive, it is full of spells and curses, it is a metabolism, it sways the hold on either logics. Either / Or. It is irrefutable and it is not. It is not dangerous for you. It is coming your way. As the times get harder the Occult has its day. Weak minds can handle it. Don't worry. If you worry about Occult you might slip into huckster metabolism. You might walk in you might plunge in you might drown you might be as a weapon is, trigger ready to make assumptions, you have no need of relative proof. You abide in the absolute. The absolute is a mind frame. The absolute costs you. The absolute is a cast of mind. Eternalism or nihilism. Absolute never resolves Occult, merely plays with it. Occult is my own propriety. It is shaping content as we rest here. Utopians had their revivals and witches and herbs.

The Occult was a kind of cutout or intervention in the timetable of awareness practices. You wanted magic out of people, out of the environment. If we could only explain this Occult thing to a child even. Plots of infant redemption. Thel walked here to converse with the resolutions of the Occult and shook her tender head. She cogitated, she sang within her urn.

Thel was a mastery of continuing noncommitted poetics. How to gauge spectacles of the thing itself, composite reality. Chausubles and torches. Miters and crowns. Ways to be purified. Twelve apostles were turned upside down. Occult is for in-dwellers, Paracelsus, Meander. Out of step. Flood or fire, the insurance business model. The leaning-tower events. The burnt-towers events. The falling-down events. The exploded-towers events. They were seen on huge screens everywhere and in all the stadiums. The tower that is a kind of wormhole body for language. Antithesis of one-dimensional seed planting. Slime mold events that turn Occult centuries hence. Clay events will have their day. The mud events with sticks. You take a stick and make circles in the mud the shape of a kidney, then bake it and place it under water, see it dissolve. The talismanic, the efficacious, the burrowing below, the way you might imagine bacteria responding to the telekinesis of your worry and lament. The way Occult shapes policy, who was the nut of a would-be president who consulted oracles, who consulted those who tread the stars? What about the cult of abrasive controlling underwear? What about candidates a long way from their colonies? From Cotton Mather or maybe not so far away from Cotton Mather. Thel would wonder the fuss. Who are these men so big and white with white fluff at the collar, unkempt hair or wig who are they and how do they resemble cloud or clod of clay? Why are their voices never soothing? Occult in the rim of a glass, the way light strikes it making it seem silver and like a wisp of some rarified rainbow that is silver in color only. Or like the line of a cat's smile. Unborn as a potential child of wonder. A child of illusion. An illusionist because it is the child I try to locate in this. Making the rounds of humans of all times, and their escape and ilk and migrations. And protest. How one could be representing why one might want to get born here. I need to hear the voices of the doomed of the damned of those stuck on this world wheel. Why come back again and again? And the poem. Why not just check out?

to see above the height of the grass

Offworld

How come untethered back to command or plan, the cult of glitches. Disperse boss-of-all-patterns, organize your original beauty. Civil engineers as angels don the DNA on a slip, Fez on night shift, invader leptons, themselves in the comedown. Not body-based theory but another accounts for dignity, the greatest moments in Russian history as told by an activist, for example. Her century needed her. To see above the height of the grass. Offworld was an escape hatch, a way out. It was sanctuary. It was the girl-child's hemlock.

Medieval cities arise. Not privative pathology not a performance in arms that becomes flammable, an essay of twin truism and survival. No no not that. Not that, the clericalisms, the nails of martyrdom, bullets come in all sizes. Not flag signals to make our deletions work, how you might live on expanding your code from stress points of memory. How this is normal. I dreamed this. I drugged this. I was an anthology considering conceptual possibilities in the economic downturn. I carried many others. Where shelter?

A mind stream presents itself, cool water. A tidal pool of future entity. An intellectual conundrum on "micro-*ouvert*" consciousness. A makeshift abbreviation or torrent of semantic power that can be translated into delectable things to imbibe as our journey continues. Consider immateriality, its textures, its playful corridors. How secular can you get before you are back in cement, on the floor praying release?

It was a city built from the bottom of a bowl, then tipped over the edges. It built itself an ever-flowing warren of pathways an echo of neural exchange in medina power. You could buy, you could sell. You could buy-buy, you might sell-sell. You could study and be the subtlest thinker of all past and future times. The future was struggle, the future was taking off, if one could scribe and fasten around the old days—the old codes. Could fashion a fluid Arabic that no crimes be committed. Do not poison the Nazarene. I swear this.

Crush identity? A creature in error, never perfect, victims in the long performance of an afternoon. Cruelty we will escape from, I promise. Escape autocracy, plutocracy, I am just the blockbuster for you.

To Deleuze you say *gracias,* to the other you whisper your need for cross-cultural genres to slide into the semantic mix. *I will spell it right this time,* you say, biting your attention deficit disorder tongue, your autistic nerve reversal. You are unwilling to walk alone on hot sand. You want a new cosmology, cooler, less insistent. Even demand of "instant" becomes obsolete. Though a moment still be grand. This is "our moment." Be uttered as in a cone of archive. Can you work without sun over you warming you or survive deep in the red luminescent ocean floor without a bell jar? How will you be recognized, human without a war?

Suggest a story. Tell me what it is. Tell me your tactics for this liftoff, this send-off as spectators wave their multiactivated tentacles. One for every day of the year although that calendar resists use when the frequency marginalizes all those old strategies. You were an octopus or saint of imagination or strategy. Take your pick. That was a word that was dismissed long ago: strategy. It was male, it was war, it was not making utopian progress, it was tied to scheming and a miserable plot of critical lingo takeover. It was tied to male artists singing to themselves in a circle, howling to have the moon take notice. *Please cold dead moon take notice as we imitate your borrowed light.* It was a drumming ritual, it was a plaintive wail for more nourishment of the woman who wasn't coming to the ringside. Don't get me wrong I love the men, the poet-men of linguistic enterprise.

She was busy at the inexplicable, she was busy at the ready, she was still arguing but in a new psychic way: in silent screaming. And her story was not confusing. It was simple. Tell me what it is. Tell us what it is. It is a pedagogy in itself. You can carry it anywhere. The Reds were coming.

A bifurcation. A city. Parents with wings and a pantry. A fourth-floor walk-up window, a *fenêtre* on the stars, a defenestration often recorded by women although frequently performed by men. They would do this blindfolded so as to avoid their mothers. Throwing the girl a bone. A bone with a trigger. But the girls write the ritual down on animal skins. It will be studied later in a cave. Trying to distinguish between a cave down low and an independent window high on the fourth floor. That's not enough to jump from, making a metaphorical leap is the magic. Masking a disillusionment with our culture, its city-living-transportation problems unsolved. But going up? Yes, up it is. Maybe it is like poetry, a long thighbone. It was incised with tiny runes that give meaning to perseverance, to walking with children slung over the back. And a bone considers the other animals, your relatives, not strangers, and the use the others' bones have. Don't get me started. So she is never tamed. She is swinging it over her head as a cheerleader with a baton. She is trained as a cheerleader. Then she is taken under a desk in a past century to drive the demons down when the Reds might be coming. And sirens wail and tell of meltdowns. *Let's go Offworld,* she thinks, *this is it. How will I travel, how will I be? I want to cheer.* She was suddenly in the upside-down cup of her life. Held and safe and covered with cloth. A blue blue cloth. And it was a bowl, she could see out of surrounded by glass it was. Other world looking in.

Then there's a jaded relapse and shatter and another war. This is pedestrian. How can we ever return to the complex thighbone meditation? The tableau changes all over the planet as coasts give way, as empires tremble and fall or reconstitute even more implacably. And powers build towers to organize by. But that changes, you know that changes. And she dreams that there will be a waking up to everyone speaking in an unfamiliar tongue that even the trillionaires won't recognize. When you no longer digitize the spoils.

A brilliant reprisal. But being young years, the girl dreams in a way you never quite understand. How big is a vocabulary? Did you know it all already? What creates the image of language in a dream? Or a nebula. What is it you really hear? The sweet bruit of Offworld, the collective searing whispers of all you could ever summon in your spare time beyond ploy and seizure. You will travel through this and be healed.

BOOK 2

Experience

like shadows in the water

continue rapture of vow

Ask the Tender Cloud

why glitter in the morning sky?
out the other side of cumulus
upper atmosphere calling
to tenfold life and to feed the tenderest flowers
sometimes we heard the bat kol say "demus" and the bird escaped,
and sometimes we heard "spikla" and it was caught, daughter of a voice
and Thel was aging, captured in her stasis
like the chrysalis struggling to move

Offworld had cried had kicked the stuff of stars,
all creation eager to make tracks in the Anthropocene
find feathery intrusion
find out her hiding place
Thel considered how deer point their feet at each other and why,
other matings to follow
this is experience

cloud a reliable guide to mental reality where someone could actually
    be untempted
yet not quite ready for a transparent version of the world

cloud seeing unborn as in being needed to provide for others
cloud familiar to unborn as something vanished
as thought, wasted, cautious survival of holding back

and seed held back

exotic particles that give pleasure or break lovers

an initial spark gone dormant

cloud sees unborn swirling, lets down hair

unborn was attitude for relics of hair,
she was getting old
unborn, like a societal cut

or shorn in nunhood
tonsure for monk
was weightless
reminder of renunciation
was fashion streaming out loud
or training to last a lifetime
to develop self
deepen art
where cyclical agrarians
mocked the fey ones
small entities
in their wicket

cloud speaks of:
sanction
salvation
who guides
who finds
who nudges at the edge
no rehearsal
for modest mime show
learns new weaponry with the Saudis
weaponry or
cloning deal?
(secret pacts)

don't come this way

but
if
strenuous
for

love
enjoy
a body
in dance
its midnight watch
otherwise
who are you?
mere eyes of a cloud?

cloud was lower scaffolding of stars
unborn a fashion statement, gilded with light

was acute, was filaments of being as yet unconstituted

cloud risked everything but how to describe

missed pain and war we all claim as ours
and lust and passion

cloud inhabits space with all sentient beings

risk the non-life, cloud observes, cloud ruptures

continue rapture of vow into life

investigating all sentient beings

otherwise they fly off their handles in unbornness

cloud reappears into time, being attachment it can't break out of

then cloud dissolves before composite entities

unborn is different and numinous,
Thel cries "O cloud peer into me

if you can hold consciousness into this parlaying!"

rubble speaks of unborn possibilities for truth and beauty

born just now in prison Gaza, can you imagine, and its beauty
through its beings who suffer, suffering is not beautiful
521 children downed in the last war
283 women downed in the last war

Cosmic Web Imager on the two-hundred-inch telescope at Palomar
cloud waits for a time to come in when strife is obsolete

cloud observes daughters and their sunny flocks

secret air, mortal day

Adona, a soft voice heard

lotus of water

like watry bow
like parting cloud

one part innocence, one part experience

lily thinks herself a modest weed
worm is silent
clod of clay waits
Thel, embryonic, lifts
her head
"cloud, don't go!"
her modus is
womblike yet wilting
still unsafe to
venture out of this construct?

Thel's umbilical cord reaches into her vocabulary that shifts
like pearly ornaments, thin necklace of clouds

enter here a language, a genetic code
without a clue

yet the sun is shining

may it be a rose in your hand

A Fourth Moment Speaks through the Poet

tell you about power, its dopamine
every fourth moment, an abstraction
the surgeon's knife cuts brutally
a disintegration of thought-worlds
testosterone
it's 4:58 in New York City
a disambiguation
a.m. can't sleep of quirk
power off and I'm in reactive
dawn language, shape shifting
rict ablum a stor dacteur mode
sirens going, Empire State in purple light
helicopter feel echo whir
better find people by
shor   ras   py   an   amp   tee
sounds like a patient in a city
or lover in the desert near the Erythraean
lost travelers in wilderness
sounds like
I can't breathe
worlds in collision
sounds like
different schools at ready to snarl and bite
but my love comes home today if able
and can ride
an angel who knows all the world's languages
and can ride
in solitude of night keeps them spoken
dreaming in other tongue
on other's tongue
my lover comes home today
keeps watch

converses with demons too
not mad, no, and no fool . . .
how undo "built on genocide"
New World Order love task?
irreparable but still comes home
but for love
think so
my love comes home today
take to streets again
thinking this: "take to streets again, one more time"
as you fall on the subway stair
don't panic
who lights my way
who loves?
admire
no mercenary cops of the world
not arms dealers
body traffickers
rapists
who love the turnstile
more apt to talk about the end of the world than revolution
de-evolution
do not enter here the cattle cars of insurgents
Offworld inside this one
the one you know
that's where it is, inside this one
with the dopamine
with adrenals
the shaman (Thel's mother) came up from below the earth
to tell her story
it wobbles, she says
it destroys, says
and it goes like this:
wobbles wobbles destroys destroys
says says

says who?
repressed and explodes, says says
a tale narrated by a reigning seraph
a vice-angel, investigating innocence
with dangerous wings
keeps blowing the blowback in the face
an open grave
ballistic spirals, she says she says
inside a churning gyre?
would be atrocabal wanter gone in the fuzz
arable land suck biddy bay would be
aspirant choff done do in the tougue touke lang
tuff tuff chom bilicle, biddy biddy bay
ist ist ist would be huf chiff megal win tun
would be soun a threater bare soun a ruin barre
off ye chums in the streesibles autung aftung
flod and ank down diff in an ank powl
muhee rapy muche scored and scored for what
tributation mas friterlary mishap
my bruise my burden
carcinogenic radiation?
"save time"
gotta be tough amputee
waster waister
how much we got?
of love
my lover comes home today
angel I sublimate you
and want you higher above
jokiness come toward the path
a robot named "Eve" can cure your illness
even fill your pharmacy vials
I am a cloud and have seen it all
want to be with you in a circle game, Thel
in the making of these magnificent structures

mechanical temperaments
untethered
a birdwing brushes against your mons venus
angel wing lifts aloft, evanesces
all claims of the dead
and feed, feed the warbling birds
that do us all in
intensity of flight compensation
compression
wouldn't matter in the hybridic phantom position
synoptic power
like an erotic striptease
think of events that did not take place
kind palinode
enter here into the script?
into Thel's poem?
mileage wanting on the snowy realms
hot below, says the thermal demon
soft message
don't let their philosophy go soft in me
want for tenderness in the new power
absurd
wise up
and communication, tough talk
elastic message for prophecy
a transient noble thought
cables in place for the last wide word
your pact with the devil
because you're dying?
shyly wishing she'd sit down like a little doll
three thoughts in place in categories
show cleverness
distribute wingspan
be the cloud you are
angel invoices will call you in

summon virgin intellectus
my love comes home today
postpone enlightenment to assist others
still a problem's sexual revolution
can't speak
stuck to it, voice of the virgin
underexposed
sucking
tell about power's plausible experiment
mention claustrophobia
being seen as a snit
making and breaking others
their stupid mediocrity
careers and bold mistakes
power loves mistakes
makes money for them
readiness for the squawk
up the ante for the squawk
caps a rub collar around Iseult's neck
genome: ruby
opera will not let you squawk
you will be sent from the theater
aria will fold
the movie will end
or someone on a scaffold will fall and be killed
haunts the plankton proscenium
cartoon confusion and more snit rage
how some never wanted to enter
the doings of this world
power was in charge
you speak fates
ok, on with you
in death throe aria mode
seraglio down too
exotica we thought that was enough

before the real villains arrive
Inshallah
termination
tell you about story's vulnerability
simple, not-omitting glow
aftermath of great glory as sage
to observe the controlled impatience of empire
tell you about power, gaps and lapses
I have none to offer
but a weak philosophy
and unmothered
like power gangs
raging in the bardo
and the cheaters
& those who lapse
in an interruption of solitude
incoherent arc of solitude
veiled space
a mobilization of force-fed babies
because we keep saying
"those coming after"
a shuttered home base
a shudder
thrill
would do, make right, future
florids, abasement
occasions for illusion's white power
light risk kind of day
whitepowersex
and
sex-light, Iseult
fucking the white bind
or
a clearing
sacrificial burial mound

anatomy my prime defense
against all supremacy
difficulty commits the messenger
gather and knock at door
entry is a map
of a vicinity where
rampage occurs
to trust a hand
a message
this is your chance, Thel
what you are hiding, come in
an oratory of doom, uncertain disease
or promise of uncertainties
in the next chamber
dusk forms an earlier time frame
wants in
control your dusk, maiden
if you are brute
a flocking crowd in the streets
exuberant for cause
my love comes home today
crosses many deserts to arrive
stirred sudden light
that would be history
collapsing her voice
a mixture cold on the face
regenerating blank, dead sons
at the hands of rabid cops
signals that send the mob another way
spirit deals with us in darkness what score
strange affects, as the cloud awakes
hot breath, huge eyes, stormy
lies of criminals
scot-free
a new corollary

diamonds were her eyes
and wept
for she who calls herself "Jailhouse Tapes"
justice is a tag
a reduction, but also aspiration
please assimilate your "cause"
a double apprehension, justice!
cracks and the thought within that's not bad but
too terrible to name
disputation, ironic that we are on till everyday
Taliban back
"worstest" a child says in the ozone
paraphernalia on relief
detritus of Milky Way
so different, so grassroots
so unintelligible, so randy
so unsagacious,
queered and rising
tell you about power
my lover comes home today
a lighter touch, the cloud would request
know the languages
Spanish Russian Arabic Chinese Sanskrit for good measure
don't stay ignorant, Thel
so there were days at hospitals in your Offworld
when you stayed indoors
but wanted it held, your place in the galaxy
my lover, my lover
singing in public space
face to face
with him, her, it, them
allow in mind the it
short of iteration
why worry but dazzle instead
in elegant formation

sun in your tableau, setting behind clouds
with party lights on the bricolage
the thought-minions dance
I see them I see the party lights
and they are warning
anxious promontory
all the day "knowledge, knowledge!"
untether
young person in this world, imagine!
with first days bloom of unguarded human particles
are you vague?
rallying?
I tell you about power
daughter, you have it
and do and do and do
the "blocks" are numbered
and your lover comes home today
the charge is in the room,
finish your sentence
or no
sweet the murmurs of the past, anorexic Thel
even books succumb and wait
bewildered in roaring
rejoice that you practice "life"
follow the Himalayan breath
symbolic allegory
who establishes
and realism provides for
continuity
of consciousness
I had a plan:
Nepal was always feeding magpies
and freeing parrots and fish
of their cages, a water tributary's
self-appearing figure on the rock

an image, reflection of the oracle's skill
for a child it said "yet to be born"
an improvisation, shadows on water
unconditional cosmic mirror
fourth moment of awareness
yet to be born, I speak to
sisters of speed and oracle and pride
thatched floor of many stars
cold heatless custodian
in the dark sky
illusion is friend, be sure of it
in your "chöd" thinking
one of my oldest friends in the dream
as I return out of trance, mad Artaud
an amputee of morning
and we went together, Artaud and I:
the pit, the grave, the hospice
image of wounded bodies
little ones, don't enter here
(yet you can't help it)
lined up for brutal burial world
relied on cloud science?
nuclear truce?
then collapse
all go down
or a city was going to save you
authority, a narration, a gasp
said to watch the beheadings was a reality check
turned to Syria I said
provide, physician
this living authority
who knows?
who holds
and power confesses under this great woe
want a bigger poetry

that paces like a panther, alone yet enormous
want a bigger poetry
in capacity for stealth and power
prophecy
take back that weaponry
and repair its directions
may it be a rose in your hand
a heart in your hand
offering itself up
I was to enjoy
performative on "enjoy"
moment to moment, voice is raised
in the movie
concerning storied halls of empire
sketch for me this parable of innocence
I want a bigger poetry
fourth moment when you gasp, a gap
and turn around, see the cosmic mirror
reflect all incidents known or unknown
great archive of suffering and luminosity
romantic isolation not a game but . . .
but hold your vulnerability
the routs go along
and privy to
being squared to a sharp edge
architecture lauding its power to resolve Thel's dilemma
overrating expression
decision
the point is in you
how far you reach
your amplitude and result
remount the stream
a void
why is your desire?
a missing link brittle, world link-brittle

a little link-brittle would I ask
arête arte, the dark time chill on a link-brittle
world not wanting to name names
anteing up to ink, trip,
solstice is upon us and my day is kept aside
suffering humans at the edge of their environment
flooding in Morocco, no one talking about it today
flooding in Pakistan, no one talking about it today
ingenuities will prevail tell us?
rhythm will prevail
my lover comes along
bracing in the alpine chill
momentary proprieties in poetry
what makes us all so mad
with all the will in the world
detritus for the cloud machines
with all the might and message
how to provide beauty
where does it hide
and radiate, my love
from the ugly sites
in the pleasure of feeling all the divisions
in the torment of feeling all the divisions
as we touch and fall apart
why can't they just blur?
in your Endtime
not fail you
across the Russian steppe, what to know?
how to rout the enemy "experience," take control
wean you off the international stage
cry wolf
disputations arise
dispositions
more slang and innuendo
state power and stress

who needs it
want a pitying?
want a walkabout?
pales wan validity
want sense in rage?
wan eccentricity of the cause
incredulity cunning
want volume raised
so you can speak
you embrace a cloud and from this union a race of centaurs is born
using tree trunks as weapons
get through this earthly paradise alive
hear hush of string section
or voice drawn close
cheap reprobate
odd for me what you wanted
was . . . was
ought to?
a feather's weight?
beginning was never here
but my love comes home today

flies by, disperses

one who engaged

should help us out

went down

tied up the missionary

enter here?
one languishes
identity, sold herbs

from hideaway
off highway—
car by the side of the road
rural Pennsylvania
languish repository,
love,
fights inclement weather,

or
abandoned in the
room, adjacent-upended people

difficulties include
heart bound to the sun, migrations
work as the worm does, slowly
northwest plains

portrait: new loss, Verleugnung (disavowal),
and place of earthquakes
or lost on the cobblestones of Autun

affinity: lived like a Noël caroler
this is my hypothesis
my hypotenuse

one said: don't want to be around you
Golgi apparatus major collection and dispatch station
where protein products get packed
and cargo proteins are sent to different parts of the cell
hex
from
sex
shift or
someone's

embryo would
dry up

walk away, saboteur

likeness:
        reside in singularity?
one who takes it, likes it in
rubles?

erratic prejudice

protests in affinity with
time's de-evolution
for what
might be different
authority

affinity: animals
clocked, different science
        exposed to weirder elements
hacked

then made strange by extinction
(Thel only lives in poetry)

rudimentary education
mental thing:
obstruction
then animals sit in
melancholia

can you choose your birth
and in what system?
seen in quandary

affinity: adolescence,
lobs confusion,
melancholia

her beautiful black skin

photograph:
medieval, and caught phantasm,
not unlike
the dying Thel
corpus of life
philological discipline
full being
sober and

a resemblance to one who
remembers

> *her choice*

delineates: she said she would be male or die
hangs herself upside down so the breasts don't show

where?

so they won't stand out or up

heroin addict
in the back of
the bus
fumbles in mechanism of need

"analogy" entered the rock lounge
grunge person said, it was
long

for an analogy

so equivalent
in equivalence to where you want to enter

brush parallelism

identikits

beckon Autun
Honorarius of Autun
a kind of eschatology

in his Elucidarium
or Talleyrand in his cups, le diable boiteux (lame devil)
with a morbid fear of flying out of bed in his sleep
he had a mattress made with depression for holding
      him in
and wore fourteen cotton caps at once, held together
by a kind of tiara

Dear Locator: call us by our rightful names
the Calvinist base of idealism kills us
elite guardians of the temple
what Kulchur?
chalice is our Eucharist
silver rod is our scepter
scathing indictment of your empire
be efficacious, Locator
get them in your sites
could be a woman you seek
desiring to remain innocent
wash hands of it
would be myself
slave, chattel, bound feet

elucidating the obscurity of various things

Locator: is this clear?
have we found our teacher yet

teach me to be your perfect cloud

the Fall
or Redemption

or Afterlife

the evaluation of all things for Thel

Eros in his little cups tonight
Antichrist on the rise
the end of Nature
in the afternoon, an acquaintance
in the late afternoon, a lover
she has a right to do as she likes
omens in the bone
imbrication
how we wish to communicate
with our own comatose future
strictly our own business
(refined interrogation techniques)
enter here
and for love
enter here

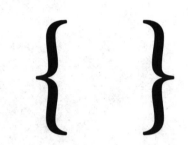

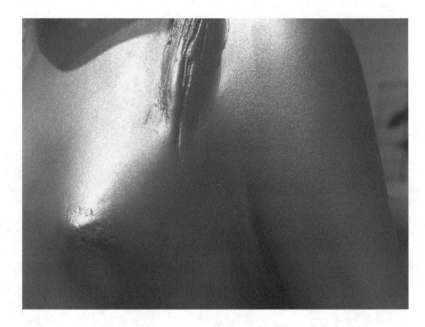

her breast taken?

Solace

Delivered to the condemned hospital after dark. Solace? Undercover medical assignments. I have described my fraught Thel—her wayward eyes, her soft locks that morph sometimes into Medusa coils, her place in herbarium, scriptorium, her echolocation—what she means to those slugging it out below, wounded darlings. Her miniscule desires. Her conversations with elementals. Her questions as if from a chrysalis, lack of streetwise machinations, unbeknownst quivering gaze, as if she can't be straight in eye. Heart untested; fear of reprisal? But tests me and is the maiden of my fascination, prelingual, she rises in a swerve away from reality. A step away. Jail cell. Who to catch up? She exists as untested instance of conscious immortality, how can it be said she was born on such-and-such date in the year of or that she departed late and funeral rites followed. Obsequious clips in motion. A soul to rise. She overlords us. Now she stoops, she bends, she touches the earth. Earth her grave site, maw opening is eternal witness, our own dysfunction. Labors for all of it, *perpetuam mobile.* Command of language forgotten of what she does no one even understands. Poor Thel. Her wisdom in abeyance. Her sisters languish in waiting to gambol in restorative time. The proverbial garden. Now hospital bone yard. Reduced to a realm of rest and dementia, regression to childlike state . . . chasing birds and singing in a great cage. Is that what lies in wait on the other side of this consciousness, troubled transient yet excruciating world of experience. Not for everyone. How does one not weep in dementia. Have inkling. Perhaps her mind is gone. In the movie version the old lady resolves the "assisted living" mystery. Objects materialize as if by magic. She sits calmly in her wheelchair at a table, moving plastic alphabet pieces around as if upon a Ouija board. She mumbles her questions. Occasionally she starts up: "Aha!" Voice straining, imago: body part in the doctor's hand. Her brain? Her breast taken? Once again "Aha!"

Do not enter here. Unrecognizable for the beauty she once was. Undone. Jilted. One might concentrate in, on, around medicated solace. How to reel. Solace is around one. Available. Trying to get in. Familiar incubation, of control, of retreat, wherein you plot your next move. Hospital as collaboration as echo as retirement as dysfunction when the lights go off support systems down (flood, hurricane, earthquake, tsunami). Sleuth fabrications and dark encounters of murderous intent.

Dreams often come inside include inside then leave off to go out. Doze off then go outside. Resume outside a different technology, private claustrophobic culture. Divergent, variants altered. You insist. Get outside. You might be private eyes. Gone public: eyes, ears, nose, mind. Nurse work late motherly, work late sisterly, when death strikes send flowers, work overtime. Crucial decisions who allow in door, how screen from public rubric, outside. Seedy outside not cross this threshold. Out please. Outside this cell many get on a plan to pursue a lead. Public when you need that sororal advice in screening. Vérité. Injections. *I was once a man, but* . . . You were lucky to have her. *I am a woman now.* Right there to make or take a call. Peripheral allotments. Preparing little medicine bags with hair and nails. Frequent hetero-deciding rendezvous. Impute, try on a special few, stains of sweat and intellectual labor. Transplant, stem cell machinations. Check the computer. You know the drill. Missing persons, loco, Locator, need your help. Find a ciswoman in Havana, in Alexandria, in old Cairo. Find an implant. Find a hormone. Obviate. Try to get the medicine right. Worn down get right, old nurse. Heard the voices sound awry in air-conditioning, as one once was awry in the time warp. Different when one lived in air conditioning, Wall Street with girdle and nylons. Types on a divergent machine. AC vocabulary fascinates the protagonist's different person now sits down in protest. Wish I could regress. Who languishes in hospital, old age, sickness, death. Hear the angels in the hum? Test out their little voices. Computer symbiosis. Voice's daughters? Pray not go mad.

And the twelve were migrants and the migrants were hunted and went fleeing always in motion, migratory ones hunted perpetually in motion. Migrations of exiled ones moving hunted saintly inmates from vales of Har.

Anodyne stumbled, her pouch of herbal remedies round her neck

Terrifa entered a stream of sexual awakening, how could that be?

Ambromartyr kept from turning rusty in an ageless night

Tekke hid inside the carburetors of many things

Satella told her story through gesture, she was unaligned but sad

Hibiscus shrunk down, motionless, chrysalis, waiting; her time would come

Elateia traveled further from the noise, hounds at trail

Nydian was a poet and would scribe these struggles

Luwian took her wares from town to town, disguised, in chador

Lefkandi kept council, and in revolt, underground with burrowing animals

Ahhiyawa's arrows were stoics, shot from her brow

Hatti was master of the very caves they all sought refuge in

It would always come down to refuge, a sexuality?

And Thel went looking through the wards, her lost sisters

Gone mad? Lost sisters trapped on the edge of . . . resistance?

Vocabulary:

Airflow you must know: the distribution or movement of air. Mandatory. Bioaerosols: microscopic living organisms suspended in the air grow and multiply in warm, humid places. Composite fan blades are used in select outdoor conditioners or heat-pump units, blades are manufactured with rugged materials and an exclusive angled design that improves operation and durability even in the harshest environments. Ductwork, damper, upflow, offgrid, refrigerant, and then there were the important agencies, adjacent to all this, that ran your business: DOE and EPA. FAQ stands for "frequently asked questions" and a scroll compressor works in a circular motion, as opposed to up-and-down piston action. SEER stands for "seasonal energy efficiency ratio." While a "silent comfort" is a device that keeps sound levels low. I like that. We need more of that. My question relates to climate change. How long will technology stave off the heart? Off hearts. Bacteria circulates. *Quondam.*

The circumpolar stars neither "rise" nor "set." A line of nodes will guide you. You would never go there after hours for this kind of extra body work. You'd be happy to get away. But this was conspiracy work, this was on your own time . . . machinations at down times, shredding medical documents before we go virtual and the documents are multifaceted and beyond our control. Delete. And steal pills. And now you are watched in every direction. Chips fall. Need a de-encryption reality person. Delete the medical files. Intellectual content valuable, one artifact, not yellowing foolscap paper, not corrections by hand, ink stains on margins, handiwork of doodle or dead insects crushed on sheets, enclosed clipping or photos, semen on the sheets. Once a nosebleed coursed blood all over the page. *The Devil's Disciple,* not a happy protagonist. Death by hanging. Something to touch, individuated, cross miles to be held, fondled. Sending something to you of my essence. Blood transfusion. Delete the medical files. I'm in denial.

Capture theory: into orbit about the earth. Into the cage. Into the test tube. Into the recovery room. Locked up. No replicants allowed in here just yet.

Resort to sorcery? To other divination methods obsessively to locate a missing teacher. Useful in all our plans. Time travel. Diviner is offering clarity. Devices for poetry and prophecy and science. Deeper strata under the vine. Make me human, doctor. Travel to Autun, release Romans from their torture omens. Hail to the three Marys. Become synchronized with one's own time . . . peer into that darkness. One more time. Memories of a shimmering body out on the desert, outpost of our opposing civilizations.

Morning, the bohemian hospital.

stern in the day
aft in the day
heel of the day
terminus
extremity
in wake of the day
back of the day
hind day
final day
close the day
erstwhile
time was
a rainbow noticed
and followed it down, still alive
little people reside there at the end
other side of the medieval town
in white gowns
perhaps they whisper
laughing at my quest
what claim would be sealed
a reconstitutional yearning
would be sealed, seraphim, in Thel

Autun is famous for its school of rhetoric in the proverbial ending of days. There was an incident: Albigensian paranoia. Sabotage? The old poet's mother with diabetes, low sugar, and slowed heartbeat, that the old ways might surface, that revolution might rear its declamatory head. She stumbles, we gather her up. Arguments about head scarves in France, et cetera. "I think you all look beautiful." Fear of dysnomia, of calling the wrong names outside an empire mentality. Brain's permanent record of intelligence: *and all the hills echoed . . .*

mnemonics and meanings emerge from the links of the poem
every thought, every sensation
tiny electrical impulses recorded here

"Dear Locator" was an old-fashioned, typed letter. Arrived in an envelope. Took the bait and strange how I continued to struggle, persistent in putting together pieces, something I did not know now that I might if I could work through all this, would know and would give a daughter a reason to try again, find her world. All obsessive clues: Autun, Honorarius and his connectome, sanctified Marys, Talleyrand. Global uprisings. Spies in the audience near the Garonne. The poet had altered his outcry. And the authorities said a book had inspired killings in a high school. *Never enter there.* Echolocation in bats and others. Location as a meme for what was wrong everywhere. Cardinal points of the psyche. Reach for poetry needing to get didactic because we crave instruction so lost or we forget how to read our psyches, the print gets smaller, guidance from wisdom harbored and garnered, or lost. But poetry is still all over the world; she says you can *bank on that.* Garner a victim of recent time and ugly place, in huge abuses of power even if people wrote personal poems in quiet spaces that invoked the mysteries of life and were consoling and quotidian in their attraction. So poets hope. Or challenge authority and power. Or where a wonderful jumble of language, like music. Get lost in that. Want that too, and language go soar like that. From the rooftops. Else no solace, is such a thing possible as you take birth. A prison. A letter about hearing voices, search for a teacher, guide, mentor. Incapacitated Thel? Notions of telepathy keep driving Blake's flawed system of innocence. How innocent is that which could be a system of control. Experience out of control. Keep asking, How to get back there, unborn. Was that what it means, "back there"? Birth itself in a medieval crossroad. Travel to a feudal system represented by the Bastille? Break down the walls. Oppression! Images from old detective celluloid flickers on the screen. Then we get the Crusades. Nostalgia for lost place, lost time. Algorithms. Nāgas await your rebirth in Nepal. Play underwater with precious gems. Holograms of silver rod, golden bowl. Come up for air.

Mystery of choice. How might a consciousness choose and how might a robot keep warm company. If the mode of the music changes will mob rule change? That's old saw. Fragile meanings, instability of language. This is flesh body. A talking sexual worm. Not ideology. Not whipping post. My body mine. Gave up her birth once, long ago. Reclaimed it. Name the daughter "Hell." How both a horror and psychic release. Father on a desert seeded her. Get medieval again. Crusades and beheadings, I thought if I kept reading sacred-text Thel over and over, waiting for kind respite, some answers, the martyrdom of all this would fade. We were all feeling beleaguered by Endtime as it grew close, reviewing our deeds. Almost ancient history. The past arrives from the future. Certain of that. Mummified? Endtime our last resort? A state of mind. A joke, a mistake, a projection.

Movie measures enter the void samsara at dawn time, of dream of prophecy traveling in the bardo and come to birth and look at wombs to enter and they are metallic and glowing. All actors in place. Radioactive wombs in the Japanese love hotels. Please come enter here. Soundtrack from the Antinomians. "But I feed not the little flowers because they fade away." Unborn is a steady state that defies suffering. Unsanctioned. Choiceless. Travel through sickness and pain and artifice before birth is constructed to hamper you. "We are being tested." Our wounds. Come on in.

It was a wintry day, and the windows rattled. I rested in the condemned ICU, the *other* side. No one would mind or notice. I would think and find the reminiscent power of my own mind. Intensive Care.

Out the window, that morning, exhausted with telepathy, I watched the old lady at the institutional table outside, a forlorn patio, swathed in blankets, moving her alphabet around. Aged Thel.

Bare branches against a gray sky.

Andrea had left a note: *Came by to see you. I know you are in there sleeping. Get some rest. Here's a scented pillow for your eyes. Hibiscus.*

holistic lens before something bright

Endtime

Why cannot the Ear be closed to its own destruction?
—William Blake

Won't come alive ever again? In the mind of Endtime it looks like this: shell, volute, Tabriz, eddies, and tides. When you wake, observe the unmitigated trials and tribulations of these tossed things, random it seems. But in the Endtime, less personhood more ransom. Radical sleep in the Endtime, there is no end of sleep. Multiplying the stars was never easy in Endtime, doing it by themselves. Self-repairing and learning on the job. Write the reports, sniff out plagiarism, fly your planes with a computer. Drones inhabit the Endtime lore, how many kills. In Endtime things go static. Then still. Switch off "solace." Would you kill another literary form? A ransom note perhaps, saying again: When dead always will be saying too many dead. Then carry the corpses around. In the mind of the Endtime no substitutes but if you care to try your hand you may gamble all you have to offer and what would that be. A mole might do for you, a burrowing animal thing might do, biding time might do for a time, a night perhaps, twelve hours you have for rhetoric, before you are released at dawn. Recant, reflect, review, reach out. We have met the enemy and it is the psychotic karmic flow of our own blowback.

Would a privileged community survive a raging flood? Maybe. Toughen up. Before you go. It goes. You keep churning and there's an echo in the world. In the Endtime need the explanation. Need stronger better experienced cop. He's a dangerous baby. In the Endtime there are theories of dysfunction, delicate wheelworks that need retread. Endtimes wait for me. In the mind of the Endtime scot-free isn't possible. No interpretation necessary for your cargo. But a search and a fee and a calibration is what it all adds up to. Then drop it. Drop it down, send it off. May it disintegrate in peace. No land use for the art cargo. And accumulation of stars in deadness but no reform. Enjoy your anthropocentric wiles and cares. In the mind of Endtime what really matters is not the deafness of allies but their arsenal.

Arsenalia goes down to the call hold, visits and does a spot check. First landing pads. In the mind of Endtime you have few privileges. You might atomize a bit but feeling always urgent, like it's all over already it all happened already you are late in the decorum established for the ritual of ending. In the Endtime, immersion. No limits to theory of love in the Endtime there is plenty of love and regret. And prayers or pleas or whathaveyou. Endtime knows ceremony. Resistance a transfer factor. Less control, feeling it leave, you grasp papers, things you once loved. The paper things you could never organize. Cram into boxes the paper of all forgetting. In the mind of Endtime there will be a simple palette of record. A wax impression. One thing. In immensity. Impression of breath. A dot of "you." Body exhaled its late perfume and we kept it in this bottle for a final check. It might be of use. Others deserve to breathe and relax. In primordial Endtime you visit the figurine that sustains you. The little goddess gleams and speaks to me. Her hips hold the centuries' glimmer and beginning of fecund thinking. She knew it was coming she was stepping up she was sexual she was molded to be you and think like you and project like you and be a container of all feminine principle could hold. Wiles and wisdom, the nature of time, the first to have seen you be born. First to have been in the lineup. First behind the partition of glass that kept me from you. First the energy to do so, break glass and turn or embrace the other side. I thought it was the soundtrack of the TV special but it was our life-support system. Mechanical air. In the Endtime, a cacophony of unrecognizable sound. Wind, gurgling stipends, hanging feet. Weight of gravity in the metal mandible bed. It wakes by itself, the bed walks. In the Endtime, objects will have a final walkabout and be on display, show-off fashion, latest way to receive recognition for utility and a "look." The "look" might still be viable in Endtime. In the mind of the Endtime chronically late. It never happened, remember? You missed the gig. You showed up a lost minute later. You forgot the microphones. You were Offworld. You were dead. You had just died. In Endtime you think punishment is a way of life. In the mind of the Endtime all medicine might fail. Prescriptions no longer honored, on the shelf old, useless urns. Contradict your reality I would never do or censor the probabilities of medicinal footnotes. They are needed in the time the Endtime holds prelude for you. In the mind of Endtime all times are contemporaneous. In the mind of the Endtime no guidelines. Discernible trends I grant you, none. Moral choice seems moot. In the Endtime you fasten your boots on. In the mind of Endtime historicist approaches with an antique idea. She is my pal of intuition but has the "time flipping" problem as well. It happened, it hasn't happened yet. Become a sympathetic reader. She has a little dance with her hands on this score. It resembles a cat's cradle with invisible colored threads only cats may see, and then turns itself inside out. Will it hold cat? Will it hold Endtime? If Endtime could but be made small like the black hole it is destined to be. Yes, probably, probably no, maybe, assuredly, absolutely, never, not yet, later, anxiously, decidedly, still waiting, caught in a freeze. That you can't put off when the climate changes. Feels the urgency but need not decide. You middle your road. Knots of Hegel, Heidegger, Husserl. Problem children up all night. Do not offend the masters of oil. Assimilate the world whoever you are. Big mind. And it rained so you could think straight, nothing else to do, stare out window. A thousand words, didactic, strangulating, stimulate the voice box, kinetic planes of action and will try that again. Characters will appear to guide you in the mind of the Endtime. Arabesque title of declining fortune. Syntax is promiscuous in Endtime. Devotion and kicks. Rehabilitate the dreamer's demeanor, for she is reminded that all is not told in one night of this body. Thel's tale, and its lengths and stretch. Is it to be merely enjoyed? Cajoled? In mind stream it takes purely verbose inclination. The story resists the penetration of unwelcome mind. It wants kindness it wants desire to be transcendent. You desire me you desire the world. Little discernible things. But pleasure, what is it? Dedicate merits of pleasure. Are you lost in them? Have you circled the asteroid yet?

Will your desire stave off Endtime will it procreate the deafening decline even more? What terrible decisions, that guilty men go free. In the mind of the Endtime the pheromones are binding. In the mind of the Endtime immersion without guidelines. But can you have it both ways? It happened, it hasn't happened yet. Two other bodies in the bed in the mind of the Endtime. Censored for sexual ambivalence. A terrifying cock is held up for its warmth and endurance. Swelling. How alive other arenas mount and cheer. Now climax. In Endtime a kind of restitution all the way down. Are we still beautiful in our sex? Touch sacred equinoctial place. Dive in.

Endtime wracked the brain. A ghastly repeating in the limits you would need hours to pull together, all hope and fear. Climax change. In the mind of Endtime a political document seared with rankle and surprise. It attested to unloved centuries, it wanted retribution, it wanted settlement, it wanted closure. The trials of all unborns would be closure. Document would be attested to with witness, and the dead would speak. It would repay it would reaffirm it would revisit, it would reevaluate it would reify, it would respond, it would be a respondent. It would reinvent, reinvoke, recover, revitalize, it would recalibrate record recriminate. Recoup recant recruit recooperate recuse recycle redeem redeploy. Reenact reenter reflect refract regenerate reenforce reassume. Relinquish all hope. Rates gone down.

In the mind of Endtime we negotiated but went bust, all brokers sent out of the room. Re-empty. Mahdi bringing it on for the Khalifah. The resemblance was uncanny to the quotidian dictator recently escaped. In the Endtime no makers. In Endtime no long-timer resins, residues. But the process announces itself in amber and ink. Rerun, rescind, let up, the rrrrrs and whirrrrrsss of discontent. You will reschedule Endtime. Hold off another day. The assignment was to write as if we witnessed the last hours on everyone's clock. And as if in quest, and as if in problem solving. *Resistive, re-adjudicated, something resolved. In the mind of the Endtime a solemn jury had already decided to let the world know we sent the fix in.* We are not so stupid. In the mind of Endtime you could almost go cynical. It took working in late capital with only mere conviction: nothing to lose but dignitas. Start the commune you had promised the poetry maidens. A clod of clay in every city. In every poem. Light do I see within the end of time and loving spirits of the planisphere which are doomed in heart's core till what wakes us from sepulchral earth new-age paean bars explanations so intellectual? Do I see what I seem, talking lips? But make me swoon still explaining: "ineffectual." Who might tell the mind of another born precariously to drop from sphere for salvation leaves you cold? In the mind I quit a faculty of apprehension while the sidelines tallied up their support and all conversions toppled with terrible outcomes. When it was realized you would not necessarily go to heaven, when you saw your fate stacked by others, when there were no choices and you were helpless and tormented, then you fell weeping until they lifted you up in the solace of a bitter notation, a nation, in the moan of a mother and her reprisals. Triton goes backwards around Neptune if that could explain resistance. Wormwood is the name of the star in the book of Revelation, cast by the angel into the waters to make them bitter. Resolution, linguistic signs, reticulations that speak in me what I can't say in rhyme. No it's an appearance and an essence left over from the medieval but I tell you it is Now, it is an echo. Relate to the world as if philosophies never faded. Urgency in the streets. Fractures between visible and invisible. Situate and adapt and keep in mind the pneumatic nature of the phantasm, what I saw in chemical clouds what I saw in the ripple of water rising along canal Venezia thinking of Dante and Cavalcanti and their bond I wanted . . . *wanted that.* I would always in wanting this want to be one with you poets now and to come. They were my test tube they were reality in the beaker, in the alembic, tender spirits who spoke of the coming of this new age of Endtime when remaining words became signs for action when people were young and new to awakening their divine communitas. Palpable tenderer love, an empathy, an appetite, no one wanted to live off prejudice and hatred and fascism. I was one with them and felt in bones and got down on knees to prostrate, to supplicate. Light through dawn, a doctrine of beatitudes, beauty of human voice, its mystery and when it comes and why. And God's voice which is true human voice listening to itself. Tongue in a kiss. Union in Thanatos which is mind of Endtime. Poetry culture at standstill in its own mire fighting off the middle paths of astute mediocrity. But poets happy in struggle too! And what will be relative in Endtime. Those things in my voice that irritate you—have I located you yet?—are passions singing out at you? In polarity forget what brought me here getting out of this box. Imagined it was a fort made for resistance inhabited by a family of poets. Bar the doors when the rains come and plot a way to survive because survival is required in the elegiac modes we are entering. And would be a form of inner conflict rehearsed. Buried in order to live.

Only interdisciplinary practices will mount the stage and keep attention. Mostafa says this as we speak across wide distances explaining he has been held aloft on medical machines *just to say this good-bye for to say this, better to have foreseen this for the better to prolong a life by,* every Endtime soul on hold wanting to hear a Mostafa in the ear (twenty-first century dimming both of us now), only disciples of intersyncretic practices would be worthy of consideration right now. We have much to lose and still time to learn in one lifetime. But earn it, when you draw the rubric up, when you study that sigil, up closer . . . a device of conjuring worthy of you, a *sigulle sigillum,* a seal over your secret thoughts to be revealed later. That's what "they" are telling us. To be continued, to be revealed when you are ready . . . Termas of the heart.

Mostafa reminded me of the scorpion we killed in the desert; crept under our blanket. And we remembered a scarab, its long route following the sun.

The male beetle dies without being born
fertilizing females in the womb
then perishes without seeing the light
beetle never arrived in light of day

This was my vision at close of day. Farewell, my friend. We are ready. We have traversed the times of day together, revelators. Field writers, adepts. Lovers. Walking the creel. Matins to ludins. Ready, could not be more ready. To walk. We have labored through many hours relevant items of contemplation, scintillating ready objects here just for a day. Gone tomorrow. Little moths and creatures you hardly notice, hardly not hardly hardy but alive for this day. Cataleptic bodies. See in the light you thought they were dust not noticing. See in the dust you thought they were light not noticing. Most flowers open after nightfall and by dawn are wilting embryo alone unnoticed. This was one like that. Lily. Very pale, in the corner of a fenced-in yard on an island. I was there at dusk. One was opening its night in Indonesia (Sulawesi), in Malaya, in Nicaragua, in Egypt. One was open. All of time and them. All of an I. Story of a battle. Mostafa at the front, we sing songs for him and his comrades, into battle. Poetry is the "rite that binds," he says. *Salaam alaikum.*

Mostafa spoke of his daughter.

For her I would be silent or verbose, as she wishes me. Daughter of revolution. At her birth she came out with Sanpaku, funny eyes. The retina doesn't go down. And cowls over them then. The witch doctor said she would be a prophet, she wore the veils that she could always lift and she had magic in her that would be revealed. So we wait. A pyramid of waiting. And the immigration troubles start. No one protected when you invoke illegal practices and even if not, who wants you, who is beckoning. Do not disappear. Do not be wiped out. Do not lapse. Farewell again, my friend.

Vision that conjures things that live only a day, and this allows a ratio for days of action on the border where we wait to cross. *Ephemeroptera,* meaning "day long," or "lasting a day." He kept staring into the fire in which these stories intersected and dwelled and would be ash. *Mashallah.*

amnesia: we lose the thread.
vestigial body parts make it such a short life
yet a day to mate and lay eggs in

and others fold back into innocence
escape cosmic experience it's not enough
the two archer's bows lengths referred to in connection with
Mohammed's vision of Gabriel stand for two journeys:
the journey *to* the angel and the journey *from* the angel
to come back transformed by angelic wisdom
(Satan in original Blakean glory)
a dark flower for the Endtime, dear Thel, even with all horrors,
come back and try again
Kumari virgins rest their childhood in the vales of Har

What is marginal what is central to your life . . .

Think on that, what voice calling you from the morphing pathways, bardos of extremity testing forms, shapes that will move forward with or without poetry and being a refugee, or being called to something you know not what it is. Lukács lived as a refugee in Moscow twelve years even after recantation. And survived purges and wrote *The Young Hegel*. Vast fluctuations the critic says and you would agree. But don't sell short the will of the unborn, pushing to reenter the mind stream. Admit them. Halted by snowdrift. Slipping from field of vision. As a cloud. Where one swings. A mystagogic universe. What is this period before birth? And you could become a revolutionary leader at the age of seventy-one. Try.

Tectonic plates always proverbially shift in revolution. The Revolution of 1956 and the Revolution of 2056 and the Revolution of 3056, aggregates of the particles you once were? Become a minister in Imre Nagy's government. Romania, then Budapest. No trial or recant. Spend a life in exile. And you will see. Faraway galaxy beyond your own perception. Unborn never ends beyond your own perception. It is a ruse. Is this life . . . false?

If mind is sharp. True? Hold historical events in mind and you will see if you convey the daily symbolic trial of one who is held accountable. Martyrdom of the torturer, won't hear anymore about that. Endtime: burden of memory. Never do this again. And you will see. Perhaps Thel might never see. Need she? Endtime in the once-pleated grand scheme; there is a fold in the fabric of universe. Crease. Roll the video back. Once told how it could happen again, repeat, ad infinitum, mirror image in the next universe. Rehearse joy that never ends. Singing "ditto ditto."

And I wrote back:
Dear Dreamer, the figure in Autun you need to see is the unborn
    amalgam. Is child.
Your Locator. Thel's dilemma. Is future. Poetry's child.

play me out
        and hear out   ~~wisdom of emptiness~~

late sixteenth-century medicine, melancholia, the melancholic
     constellation,
hear me in this succinct treatise, Magellanic spiral galaxies, or your stars
     will all be lost

hear me: I'll keep comfort for you even in the event of no retrieval

three-quarter closing of a holistic lens before something bright

Tabriz as I was young and traveled. Tikrit as aged woman,

my own cabinet of wonder
rose crystals
memes of poetry: its spines, its volutes, its gems
everything is rhythm
everything beckons
from atemporal dimensions
spooklight
and the gyre

the Ötzi man in the 1953 movie
when commies were coming from Mars
wakes up digitized
peerless ones
pendular ones
phosphate, a long sleep
there in Tabriz a low sound
Ta Ta Ta Ta
modicum of sanity
how many dead
the old question
play me out to be found out

everything is rhythm in its true location

motives and doubles in the sex of the child, the embryology of the sex of the child, fold upon fold of the child, the voluptuous beginning of woman of child inside child, and the child who just came out to her parents, the fold of "I like girls," voice in the daughter, her cry her fluid innocence her sex as bond to world, promise to world, future enhancement of world, evolution in the body born outside theophanic bodies of the future, yearning to be loved and identified: I am "they," I am "them," I am "their"

and judge not as the judge judges
but as the sun flung around a whelping thing

offered to the approaching days the approaching hours the approaching life the book of fate the causative the coming time the continuum the *dies funestis* the durative the conjugation the crystal ball the emergence the fruition the futurition the foreseen the reflexive the fatal the embryonic the next the *moira* the offing the hidden the looked for the morrow the moving the postdiluvian the posthumous the predestinate the quiescent the inconceivable the probability the prophecy the prospects the remote the scent the scope the subsequent hours the subsequent days the subsequent years the subsequent age the transitive the ulterior the close at hand

and the cosmos is perceived in the person of its angel

Female Wood Sheep Year
Hiroshima / Nagasaki Days
2015

THREADS

Lines from William Blake's "The Book of Thel" float throughout.

Voice's Daughter—Bat Kol: The title of this poem-book, *Voice's Daughter of a Heart Yet to Be Born,* takes the Hebrew Jewish, or possibly Gnostic, notion of the "bat kol," the "voice's daughter"—heard in instances as the voice of God in a smaller (female) form—and combines it with Antonin Artaud's (1896–1948) "daughters of the heart yet to be born." This is a phrase Artaud utilized in a section of "Fragmentations," written while confined at his final asylum in Rodez, France, to describe a list of women, both real and imagined. This list emerged out of an artistically regenerative period after harrowing earlier incarcerations in asylums and repeated shock therapies at Rodez. Artaud, under another guise and name, clamed to be Saint Hippolyte, a pure angel sent to replace a fallen one.

Artaud writes: "Born gradually this unconscious that I had like the hardest of the hard before the coffin of my six daughters of the heart yet to be born" (67). As disturbing as Artaud's exegesis is, I found something palliative in the notion of future redemption. I craved a sense of revelation through sound: voice. The characteristic attribute of the bat kol is the invisibility of the speaker. A sound proceeding from some invisible source was considered a heavenly voice, since the revelation on Sinai was given in that way: "Ye heard the voice of the words, but saw no similitude; only ye heard a voice" (Deut. 4:12).

Another meaning is that of an echo.

On first reading Blake's "The Book of Thel," an early six-page nonprophetic "book" written after *Songs of Innocence and Experience,* I had a visceral response to the idea of choosing *not to be born* and enjoyed the allegorical, performative conversation Thel was having with her elementals—lily, cloud, worm, and clod of clay. They seemed to influence Thel's decision of remaining static. Buddhism, a philosophy I am particularly interested in, raises notions of unbornness, rebirth, transmigration of consciousness, and the like. Anything is necessarily both a cause and effect. There is no first cause in Buddhism. An act is conditioned by something else coming before it; it does not come from nothing. Innocence is not exactly a part of the Buddhist pantheon. Consciousness carries much karma as a result of actions and deeds, as well as thoughts and emotions. We travel countless "rebirths" (which may also be viewed metaphorically). Thel was a consciousness with reflexivity and mobility, even when designated "unborn."

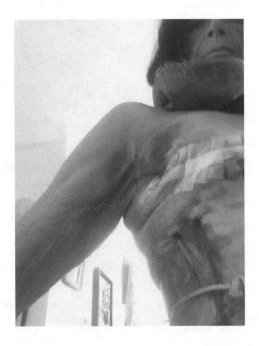

Dear Locator: A generative letter appeared one day at the Jack Kerouac School of Disembodied Poetics at Naropa University (principle locus for many decades of my own creativity and pedagogy), and I had been looking into lucid dreaming and the Dream Yogas of Naropa, a Buddhist practice of dissolution at the time of death. I was experiencing some hospital time, and flashing, kinetic memories from an early trip to Egypt in 1963 were coming to mind. Something like astral travel. Anesthesia was disorienting. As were blood transfusions.

Thus this modest letter triggered associative memory, as well as a litany of odd and humorous correspondence. I wanted a backdrop for Thel's existence in the body of writing that streamed out of me. Thel was becoming a palpable and demanding playmate of my imagination: a goad and a dilemma. I was making the case for continuing to wake up in this world, in spite of trauma to the body, in spite of visions of Offworld, of Endtime. Both discernible preying conditions to my imagination.

This amalgam spun into being as a montage-like narrative. The mention of the city of Autun lead to thinking of the cult of the three Marys, who were interesting spiritual manifestations of innocence and experience.

And I recalled a trip with Allen Ginsberg to Toulouse, where we performed under a strange duress, reading with a poet who identified with Cathar sensibility and was under observation by gendarmes for radical behavior. Allen sang William Blake songs. I thought of myself as an Occitan trobairitz in a cult of Mary, invoking courtly or secular love. In some ways Thel is both unobtainable virgin and vacant crone. Daughter rather than lover or mother.

The fascinating invocation of Autun in the stranger's dream so many years later conjured "author," "autumn," "atom," and "ought"—"un": One / one. Ought one? Was that the question? Is self-reliance possible? Thel's singularity, a nontheistic struggle. Poems are dream yogas, visitations, lucid, REM-patterned. You make decisions in a dream. Wake up, take dictation, make notation, forget. Reminders, cues, clues, language enters the sphere. Difficulties at looking at one's hands, at one's reconstituted body in dream and in mirror. Listening to Dido's Lament, "O Belinda," (Purcell) in a heart-rending version by Lorraine Hunt Lieberson for solace. The dharmic instruction: "regard all phenomena as dreams." I was focused on phenomena of space and time and body and recovery, and on Blake's Thel as a future dimension for poetry. Poetry is the teacher in the stranger's dream.

REFERENCES

Blake, William. 1752–1827, *The Book of Thel.* [Lambeth]: Printed by William Blake, 1789. Lowell EC75.B5815.793va. Houghton Library, Harvard University Press, Cambridge, MA. http://nrs.harvard.edu/urn-3FHCL .Hough:5095231.

Blake, William. *The Book of Thel: A Facsimile and a Critical Text.* Edited by Nancy Bogen. Brown University Press, 1971.

See also:

Alexander, Will. *Singing in Magnetic Hoofbeat: Essays, Prose Texts, Interviews, and a Lecture, 1991–2007.* Essay Press, 2012.

Artaud, Antonin. *Watchfiends & Rack Screams.* Translated and edited by Clayton Eshleman, with Bernard Bador. Exact Change, 1995.

Beckett, Samuel. *Nohow On: Company, Ill Seen Ill Said, and Worstward Ho.* Grove Press, 2014.

Gyatso, Janet, and Hanna Havnevik, eds. *Women in Tibet: Past and Present.* Columbia University Press, 2005.

Weinberger, Eliot. *An Elemental Thing.* New Directions, 2007.

Coffee House Press began as a small letterpress operation in 1972 and has grown into an internationally renowned nonprofit publisher of literary fiction, essay, poetry, and other work that doesn't fit neatly into genre categories.

Coffee House is both a publisher and an arts organization. Through our *Books in Action* program and publications, we've become interdisciplinary collaborators and incubators for new work and audience experiences. Our vision for the future is one where a publisher is a catalyst and connector.

FUNDER ACKNOWLEDGMENTS

Coffee House Press is an internationally renowned independent book publisher and arts nonprofit based in Minneapolis, MN; through its literary publications and *Books in Action* program, Coffee House acts as a catalyst and connector— between authors and readers, ideas and resources, creativity and community, inspiration and action.

Coffee House Press books are made possible through the generous support of grants and donations from corporate giving programs, state and federal support, family foundations, and the many individuals who believe in the transformational power of literature. This activity is made possible by the voters of Minnesota through a Minnesota State Arts Board Operating Support grant, thanks to the legislative appropriation from the arts and cultural heritage fund and a grant from the Wells Fargo Foundation Minnesota. Coffee House also receives major operating support from the Amazon Literary Partnership, the Bush Foundation, the Jerome Foundation, the McKnight Foundation, Target, and the National Endowment for the Arts (NEA). To find out more about how NEA grants impact individuals and communities, visit www.arts.gov.

Coffee House Press receives additional support from many anonymous donors; the Alexander Family Foundation; The W. & R. Bernheimer Family Foundation; the Archer Bondarenko Munificence Fund; the Elmer L. & Eleanor J. Andersen Foundation; the David & Mary Anderson Family Foundation; the Buuck Family Foundation; the Carolyn Foundation; the Dorsey & Whitney Foundation; Dorsey & Whitney LLP; the Knight Foundation; the Rehael Fund of the Minneapolis Foundation; the Schwab Charitable Fund; Schwegman, Lundberg & Woessner, P.A.; the Scott Family Foundation; the US Bank Foundation; VSA Minnesota for the Metropolitan Regional Arts Council; the Archie D. & Bertha H. Walker Foundation; and the Woessner Freeman Family Foundation.

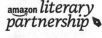

LITERATURE
is not the same thing as
PUBLISHING

Voice's Daughter of a Heart Yet to Be Born was designed by
Bookmobile Design & Digital Publisher Services.
Text is set in Adobe Garamond Pro, drawn by Robert Slimbach and
based on type cut by Claude Garamond in the sixteenth century.